What About Money

What is it? And What's it For?

by Scott Dion

Printed in the United States of America

First Printing, 2022

ISBN 978-1-7330910-2-2
Print Edition

Privacy Press
36 Center St., Suite 265
Wolfeboro, NH 03894
www.PrivacyPress.net

Table of Contents

Introduction

Even if you think you know what money is and what it's for you may be surprised to find that the basic presumptions made about its nature, by virtually all, has caused them to climb aboard a treadmill they are unable to stop. In "What About Money" I will show how our current Debt Based Money System was designed purposely to milk the majority and enrich its designers. Discover the design behind the seemingly chaotic economy and what you can do to get off the treadmill.

Let me cut through all the complicated jargon usually spewed out by economists to explain economic conditions. By demonstrating the various methods used to place Money into circulation you will learn which methods are honest and which are dishonest. Debt Based Money systems create debt and Wealth Based Money system creates wealth. Learn which one we are currently living under and what choices you have.

Continue on through these pages and stop being taken advantage of and get off the treadmill. Gain a vision for how Honest Money can increase the wealth and happiness of you and your family and the country as a whole.

CHAPTER 1

What About Money

What about "Money"? What is it? And What's it for? Money in practice can take many forms. In the past, and in some places still, it has been known to take the form of rocks, gems, gold, silver and various other metals forged into various shapes, sizes and weights. It has been bear claws, sharks teeth, shells even cigarettes, bullets, and furs. Today, it's largely thought of as the various currencies of world governments. Textured specialized paper with pictures of dead Presidents, containing numbers that supposedly represent its value.

All the items listed above and many more have been used as money but none of them in and of themselves is "Money" itself. People work for it, chase it, have been known to lie, cheat and steal for it. Some hoard it save it or spend it and some even love it and worship it. Few can do without it and most of the world are slaves to it. Yet few people know what it is or what it's for.

Take the so-called "Dollar" bill, today's Federal Reserve Note. If I spend a lifetime working for it and saving it and I fill a room in my house from floor to ceiling with it, at the end of the day, what is it worth? I can't eat it, I can't wear it, I can't build a shelter out of it. I could hardly keep warm feeding a fire with it for more than a couple of nights. It doesn't hardly seem worth the fuss then does it? Even if we were still using bear claws, cigarettes, and bullets or fur, I am not sure whether I would be thrilled to have worked a lifetime for a room full of those items either, but I could probably find more uses for them than I could for the colored paper.

So, now, after determining that this colored paper isn't worth a lifetime of labor, I'm informed that its value isn't in the paper itself, but in the fact that I can buy labor and good things from others with it! But "why?" I ask, if I have discovered it isn't worth exchanging my labor or my good things for a pile of colored paper, haven't they? Apparently not. Wouldn't I be taking advantage of them? They don't seem to care. Everybody's doing it. Maybe they haven't figured it out yet? Oh, well maybe it is like the card game Old Maid; the last one holding colored paper instead of goods and property when they figure it out will be stuck with the paper?

So the only thing making this colored paper we are calling "Money" worth anything, is people's trust and belief that the next guy will want it or be willing to accept it for the same value and things I've taken a chance on? So, is that why it doesn't matter if we use colored paper, bear claws or bullets as long as everyone else agrees to do the same? Wouldn't that make "Money" more of an "Idea" than a "Thing"?

If "Money" is indeed an idea that makes use of a material thing as a representation of the intangible idea, then does the material thing or item used make any

2

difference as to what is used? I propose that it makes a great difference what material is used to "act" as "Money" and for numerous reasons.

First however, Let's explore a little further to see if "Money", as an idea, answers the question "What is Money?", that I initially proposed. Short of my arguments to be made for one material thing over another for use as "Money", we have seen that numerous items over time have been used. This seems to confirm "Money" is not one particular item known by all people to be this idea or that such as a tree, a car or a plane might be. That "Money" is an idea and a concept separate from the particular item or commodity used to represent it is made apparent by the invention of the Computer.

Today "Money" can be held as electronic bits nothing more than a system of bookkeeping entries keeping track of credits and debits, offset mathematically with other credits and debits, having no physical commodity at all being called, or representing the "Money" itself. A Person's labor or goods production could be credited electronically as some numeric amount arriving at the new "Money" balance. "Money" in this case represented simply as the difference between credits and debits and a person's "Money" being the remaining balance. Whether that balance is described in terms of dollars, bits, cents, or drachma, is neither here nor there, as long as it is commonly understood by the participants. Although most would be surprised to know that a colored piece of paper with the numeral one written on it is not really a dollar as so commonly referred to.

A "Dollar" was originally a specific number of grains of gold, as an equivalent in a gold coin. In other words it was a specific measure. Just like a yard is a yard, and a pound is a pound, the world around. What today, are referred to as "Dollars", have no relation to any proportional measure. The Treasury can print a one dollar bill for about two cents, and a one hundred dollar bill, for the same two cents. With your eyes closed try to pick out the difference between a one, a twenty or a one hundred dollar bill. Almost impossible! But take a coin that is one ounce of gold and one that is a half ounce. Can you tell the difference with your eyes closed? In a second, it's easy.

Although this is an argument for one material over another, as better or worse, it also shows that whatever can be made to be accepted, can serve as "Money's" Representation. Therefore the acceptance of the "Idea" of "Money" seems to be its main attribute, over that of the actual commodity used, such as metal or paper. This leads me to conclude that "Money" is an idea or concept used and represented by some selected material as a "Medium of Exchange" and or store of value. If that is what it is, what's it for?

Originally, when men were few, and societies small, all participated in acquiring and providing themselves the necessities of life. Labor and goods were easily exchanged directly with others nearby, for the labor and goods of others. As populations and wealth increased, a "Medium of Exchange", became necessary whereby purchasing power could be stored for future use and a division of labor could be accomplished. After all, although you may agree to provide your neighbor with wood that you chopped in exchange for corn that he grew, at some point it would be more convenient to have shoes and a coat rather than more corn. By receipt of a "Medium of Exchange", Money such as silver coins, for your chopped wood, you could then receive not only the goods (corn) of the neighbor you chopped the wood for directly, but could take that "Money" and use it to receive a share of the goods (shoes & coats) actually produced by another you didn't have a direct exchange with.

This creation of the idea of money and a medium of exchange led to a better life for all. Rather than each family needing to work 16 hours a day to provide themselves with all the necessities of life, each could develop their specialties and exchange those with others producing different items. So by growing the food for many, another was able to tailor clothes for many, and another build homes, all working somewhat less, and still able to have all the necessities through exchange. The larger the exchange system, the more necessary the "Money" to represent the crediting and debiting each was due in the system or economy. Ultimately leading to not only necessities but luxuries and leisure in reduced hours needed for each to produce all the necessities previously duplicated by every family.

So "Money" is an idea for the purpose of building wealth and leisure and providing the necessities of life to increasingly more and more people simultaneously. So why do we still have poor and destitute people? Why, is life is not getting better and better and easier and easier? Could it have something to do with the material commodity used as the "Medium of Exchange"? What should be used to represent "Money"? Is that the problem? What about "how" its administered, or "who" administers it?

Let us look first at "What is used?", as stated previously many different commodities have been and still are used to represent "Money". Many certainly better and worse than others. Certain qualities, regarding the Medium of Exchange used, may make one material better than another for one reason and less desirable for a different reason. The important qualities and features desired by most systems include: One, that the material used be durable, two, that it be easily recognizable, three, that there is sufficient quantity, but not an overabundance, and four, that it has some intrinsic value or desirability in and of itself.

When considering these attributes it is clear that some of the items previously mentioned fit one or two of the desired qualities well, and the others, not so well. Those materials that have been chosen to fit closest to the desired attributes most often sought out, history will attest, has been the coining of gold and silver, and to a lesser extent, other castable metals such as copper, brass, and nickel in various degrees and mixes. Although shysters and thieves have always sought to gain by dishonest means, such as shaving coins, or falsifying weights, or pureness, no system has led to such outright corruption and thievery as the introduction of paper money.

The use of gold and silver in combination with each other although still prone to corruption, control of the supply by government or the few in some jurisdictions, still offers the best chance of a stable economic environment. To date they have best met the qualities sought to serve as "Money" or the "Medium of Exchange". These materials are durable and transportable they are easily recognizable, also they are of sufficient quantity without being too easily produced, and therefore have intrinsic value in themselves. The mining and preparation of them require labor and effort for any producer whether private, government or public. They offer a store of value both in the present and for the future.

The only real means to manipulation is by control over the supply and demand of these commodities to the market as an exchange medium. But this is true of any medium used to date. Yet other materials such as paper have many more problems both fitting the qualities and features for a good medium as well as having a host of methods for manipulation beyond just the issue of supply.

The first Bank frauds committed years ago, when gold and silver were largely the medium of choice were committed by Bankers who discovered an exploitable tendency of their customers to trade or negotiate their gold Deposit Slips rather than withdraw the actual gold or silver. The First Banks were for the purpose of Safe Guarding an individuals "Money" (gold and silver) from the possibilities of loss from thieves and bandits on the road during travel. This also eased the burden of carrying the weight involved. After a time, merchants, during a business transaction, would pay by signing over the Deposit Receipt, rather than extracting the gold from his Bank. The recipient could show up at the Bank and use the receipt to claim his due. Often however, the same receipt would be passed along again. The continued passing of receipts rather than the actual gold or silver led the Banker to notice he could "Borrow" from the Bank's Vault, because a certain percentage or storage amount always seemed to be available in store. Over "borrowing" of course would eventually lead to scandal, and bank run which in turn would find the guilty hung from a tree. Unfortunately today the Bankers have managed to make a so-called "Legal Monetary System" out of these same tendencies and the legalizing of paper money called "Fractional Reserve Banking".

Over the years, the Bankers have not only managed to make paper money "legal", but they have managed to disconnect that paper money from any value system associated with or regulated by gold and silver. Not only is paper less durable, it is abundantly available as a cheap commodity. (Not necessarily to us the people.) A certain cloth-paper combination highly regulated along with other security features to prevent counterfeiting supposedly helps regulate supply. But to the producer only pennies per dollar bill or even 100 dollar bill. It has no intrinsic value of its own. Is redeemable in nothing but another one of itself. The only "Medium of Exchange" quality it retains is easy recognition. The only value that it has is in its continued acceptance by an ignorant populace with little other choice than to hope in its continuous acceptance.

So now we should be able to see that "Money" is an idea represented in a material and it is for using as a "Medium of Exchange" for the creation of wealth and leisure by allowing an equitable exchange for goods and labor among the people. It is the exchange of goods and labor that creates wealth. The accumulation of wealth should be equated with the increase of goods and property and leisure time. Not with accumulation of the "Medium of Exchange" itself (Money). Although a proper Medium of Exchange such as gold and silver should allow for a store of future value placing faith in paper money to accomplish that same end is a fools errand.

The fact that gold and silver, in fact any metal, or even bear claws, make a more equitable and less corrupt Medium of Exchange than paper is found in the effort and expense of obtaining one material over the other. Paper cost the producer of it little to nothing to obtain and even less to place the number one, five, ten or 100 on to it. Where gold or silver take time and labor to mine and refine. Would you prefer to exchange your corn, furniture or cloth, produced with much sweat and many hours, with the miner of gold and silver, who also sweat and spent time, or with a person who wrote a number on a piece of paper?

Even a government or other Corporate Group who

corruptly took control of the means and supply of gold and silver to control and manipulate the supply and demand of the Exchange Medium would at least have to overcome the requirement to labor and the expenses of production and thereby have at least some stake in the game. But allowing the supplier of the "Medium of Exchange" to use paper money redeemable only in more paper is to place the chains of slavery on your own hands and feet. To allow these same demons to additionally charge interest on this so-called "Money" boarders on insanity.

"A little dramatic", you say. "Exaggerating the issue some to get the point across", you think. Not at all, in fact words alone cannot condemn them strongly enough. It is shear ignorance of the majority, to that which so burdens their lives, that prevents revolution and the hunting down of the foxes and wolves involved. If ignorance is not the cause then men have become cowards who hate themselves, their families and their Country.

Let me illustrate. Imagine you own the only Printing Press for Money and are awarded the job of keeping the Country supplied with "Money". Money which is needed to grease the wheels of commerce. So here you are with a press that for the cost of a few cents each, you are able to print ones, fives, twenties, fifties and hundreds. One as cheaply as another. You can imagine if you print too much too fast that the price demanded for the goods the money is spent on will go up quickly. The owner of the good will want his fair share of the Money floating around for his item. You also find that if you don't print enough Money, the price of goods drop rapidly because in order to compete for the few dollars existing, the seller of a good needs to lower his price the most to attract the few dollars there are.

So, you begin conscientiously trying to maintain a steady flow making Money just plentiful enough to keep transactions occurring regularly without inflating or depressing the normal price of goods. Of course, your life is a dream come true, knowing you can print yourself a few extra hundreds as cheaply as a one or a five. If you don't go overboard, few will notice as you become richer and richer not having to bother with the drudgery, time and effort of those who need to exchange a full hundred dollars of value in labor and goods for a hundred dollars of Money. You can, with the effort and labor equivalent to earning a few cents, earn hundreds.

Before long it dawns on you that if you can pass on the printing press to your children that in a few generations they could own and control everything. After all who could out bid them for anything. They will have so much they could give it away. No! Instead, it could be sold over again. Even better, why wait generations, when you could just buy more now and start selling it to those who can't buy their own today, by letting them pay you later; after they have earned what they have coming. That way their Money will become yours again before they even earn it in the first place. Heck, you could even charge a few dollars for the privilege of being allowed to pay later and call it interest.

It would not take long for you to notice that this power of the Printing Press would win you friends and influence people. Those who disagreed with you could be left out and restricted from the privilege of paying later. In fact, you could revisit your early lessons regarding printing too much too fast, or not enough, to rethink how that might be used to your advantage.

One idea might be to print a lot fast and cause some inflation while creative people with ideas would start businesses and hire laborers and produce much real wealth. Then you could suddenly halt the printing press and cause many layoffs and business failures. Prices of everything would go down, except maybe necessities. Goods would be available to you for pennies on the dollar. People making time payments for long periods of time would default and all their goods and property would revert back to you, the lender. Owning it all you could start the printing press back up and start people attempting to buy it all back from you again. Imagination hey? A good thing it is not true right? If you had this Printing Press, would you give it away?

Well believe it or not "We the People" had such a Printing Press but on the verge of Holiday Break, a small group of traitorous representatives in December 1913, with passage of the Federal Reserve Act gave the Press away. They shirked their duty to coin and regulate the value of our Money and continue to this day doing the same. With no power to audit or control the Printing Press was given over to a group of mostly European Bankers, the heads of which make up the Federal Reserve Board. These Bankers made short work of disconnecting the Money Supply from gold and eventually totally disconnected from silver and the redemption of anything of value other than one piece of paper redeemable for another piece of paper. To add insult to injury they added to the evil of worthless Printing Press Money, the additional horrors of Interest, Fractional Reserves, and the method of Lending into Circulation.

Interest is otherwise called usury and for good reason. Most people claim they dislike it when others use them. What could be more like being used and using people than charging interest? When you lend something to someone you expect it to be returned certainly, but should you expect an item returned along with another item or more items than you lent? If your neighbor comes over and borrows a loaf of bread, do you expect him to return one and a half loaves? Does it somehow insure the one will be returned if you require more than one in return? If you trust he will return what was borrowed, then your trust is not in the interest, but in the person. If you require something more in return, it is not lending, it is renting. If someone is indeed in need, then interest is taking advantage of the needy and causing greater need. In the example of our Printing Press, where the Printer is exchanging cheap paper for valuable goods and labor, is it necessary that the Printer's gain be even greater by adding interest?

But if cheap paper off a press for valuable goods and services is not ridiculous enough, then let us add interest. If we really want to be crazy, let us institute "Fractional Reserves" so our "Printing Press Owner" can allow his close friends to make some "Money" out of thin air also! If you thought your own Printing Press was wild, then you will love this.

Seems our "Printing Press Owner" is so busy doing his own thing he doesn't want to take time or profits out to pay his Banker friends, so he lets them get theirs from a system of "Fractional Reserves". This magic works by allowing them to lend or invest all the "Money" deposited in their Banks, other than a small Reserve amount. So, despite the fact that they offer you a Demand Account in their Bank, meaning you can take your deposit back out on demand, they are allowed to loan 90% of it out again. This Money is lent at Interest of course. Interest they receive on your deposit, not their own Money. It gets better, for them. When this loaned Money is placed in the person's account who took the loan, his Bank gets to loan 90% of that deposit. But wait! Isn't that the same Money you deposited, and has already been lent?

In other words, you deposit, say $1,000, so supposedly the Bank is holding your $1,000 that you can come back and get at any time. But they also loan $900 of the assets now in their Bank (Your 1,000) to someone else. That person takes the $900 loaned to him and places it in his Bank, which in turn takes 90% of this new deposit and loans out $810 to yet someone else then that Money deposited elsewhere has $729 loaned out and the 10% held in reserve. This goes on for up to over 75 smaller increments until ten times the original deposit ($10,000) has been loaned out against the original $1,000 deposit. This allows the Banks to enjoy receiving interest income on $9,000 of phantom Money never really deposited.

Most people are under the impression that they pay interest to borrow other people's hard-earned Money and that they are taking a chance on loaning it to you. Nothing could be further from the Truth. If it were the case, why then would the lion's share of interest go to the Bank instead of the depositors?

The same charade takes place when you take a mortgage to buy a home. Again, most think they are borrowing other people's money and feel obligated to be responsible and pay it back with interest. But what really occurs is no different than when you make a deposit. When you deposit say, $1,000, into your Checking Account, the Bank gives you a deposit slip and on their books they show the $1,000 as an asset held by the Bank. They also mark $1,000 as a liability because they are responsible to allow you to write checks against your Deposit Balance for that same $1,000. They do the same thing with your mortgage. When you sign a Promissory Note it becomes a Negotiable Instrument, the equivalent of Money, just like your $1,000 the Banker deposits this as an asset on his Books and marks a liability entry for the same amount so payment can be made to the home seller. But unlike the $1,000 deposit the Banker neglects to give you a deposit slip showing you *your* credit and unlike with the $1,000 deposit, when you are done writing a $1,000 worth of checks you are back to even. With the mortgage, they let you believe you still owe them the Money back, plus interest. Even if the Banker could justify a fee for facilitating the transaction, where do they get off charging you interest on your own deposit? They loaned you nothing of their own.

This whole system would be evil enough if it were just the Owner of the Printing Press having the advantage of spending the Money printed, that cost them little to nothing, into circulation as they saw fit. But the way they have chosen to lend it into circulation rather than spend it into circulation increases the corruption tenfold.

After handing away the Printing Press, how much worse could it be than that? Much worse! First let us look at printing and spending. As bad as it is to allow someone the right to print our Money and spend it for valuable goods and services which they are not giving equal value in return for, it is much worse to let them loan the Money out. As bad as a system of printing and spending is if the Government itself retained the possession of the Press at least when they spent the Money into the economy for valuable goods and services provided by the people and their businesses, the functions of government would be paid for without the need to tax its own people further. (more than the receipt of virtually free goods by having the printing press) Additionally the Government, hence in America, the People, would remain debt free. The Government, having spent the Printed Money rather than having borrowed it! Beyond that the people would then use the Money spent into circulation by the Government as their needed "Medium of Exchange", necessary to transact business between themselves. If the Government restricted their spending in proportion to the Gross National Product (the production of new wealth by the people), despite its inherent unfairness, most would be living a Utopian dream compared to what takes place today.

There would be no National Debt because Government would be paying its way as it went. There would be no need for taxing its own people since its need for revenue is provided in its control of the Printing Press. If it wanted to provide higher education to everyone desiring it, interest free loans could be given to students who performed to a certain standard. For that matter, the same could be done with home loans, etc. However, there is great danger in allowing any government to carry out functions other than the administration of law and order and the protection of the people and our Country.

Invariably whenever any such suggestions approaching the above ideas or suggesting government should own the Money Press or coin and set the value of our Money as called for by our founding fathers in the Constitution for our Country, a great cry of foul goes out. Those who currently have the Printing Press in their clutches (Private un-American Bankers) and have used it to buy most of our politicians and all our media outlets, begin an outcry to instill fear and confusion. They then remind us how undisciplined our politicians are and claim how such an idea would lead to wild uncontrolled overspending by Government and runaway inflation. They claim the Printing Press needs to be kept out of the hands of politicians to keep them from using it for political ends.

These very bandits are doing every one of the things they claim will occur, already themselves. We already have overspending constantly, only now, we not only spend it, but we also borrow it first, then spend it. So instead of owing nothing back at the end, we now owe it all back and with interest besides. Instead of them being our politicians and representatives, they have become theirs. Sure, we get to vote between A and B, but they provide us with what there is to choose from. They tell us what we should worry about, and the two sides of each issue we can choose from to be on. The only Presidents that have publicly advocated for Government control of its own Money Supply have died in office; they were Lincoln and Kennedy. I offer no theory.

When you come to see the vast fortunes, control and power wielded by controlling the Money Supply as it is handled by loaning it into circulation rather than even spending it in, you will understand why some are willing to say and do anything to maintain it.

When you simply spend Money into circulation, the Printer acquires goods and services for less than a fair value; a great advantage, but the end of it, once spent. The spent Money becomes the Medium of Exchange for the people, and they also can gain in wealth, albeit at a slower rate than the printer. Loaning into circulation, however, not only gets the Printer goods at an advantage, but serves as a mechanism to have all the Money in circulation due to be returned over and over again to the Printer who lent it. Which means it can and needs to be lent out again for the populace to even have a Money Supply and a Medium of Exchange.

Therefore, both new printing, and loan returns need to be loaned again and again. As if this was not evil enough, they add interest to that which is loaned. So, if $100 is loaned out at 10% interest, that means $110 has to come back to satisfy the loan and interest. But how is this possible. If $100 is printed and lent out, how can $110 come back when only $100 has been printed in the first place? It cannot, not without the interest also being printed and also being lent out. But then where does the interest on the extra $10 that was also printed and lent out come from? Yes, a continuous cycle, conundrum or catch 22. This alone, never mind the fraud of Fractional Reserves, changes a license to steal into a license to rape, pillage and enslave all. The Printer of the Money under these circumstances, cannot help but eventually own all property, indebting all people and ruling the World.

"Here he goes again", you say. "Paranoid, Conspiracy Theory Nut, tin foil hat stuff". But I ask you, "Do you advocate fraud? Larceny? Slavery?" No! Then why do you watch it occurring without complaint? How so?

Let us reduce the millions of daily transactions, people buying, selling, borrowing and paying from such a large macrocosm to a small microcosm of just a few. When someone cannot pay their bills, defaults on a loan, or goes bankrupt, do you think of them as a deadbeat or a poor money manager? Remember half the people are below average.

To our microcosm. Let us say, you and your family

along with two other families arrive here in the new world by boat. You stake out a track of land, cut tress, build a home, clear a field and plant seed. Life is hard and the hours are long. Each family provides for themselves all the needs of life; food, shelter and clothing, with little time for anything else. After a time, a man who says he is a Banker comes along and explains to you the virtues of an idea he calls Money. He explains how if one family took care of all the farming, another the building and another the clothing, how all would be provided with all the same things they previously did for themselves, only they would now have more free time for family and other pursuits.

He proposes to lend you some of his Money and loans each family $100 at only 10% interest. After all, it's only fair he gets something for his Money and the risk he is taking. He explains how signing a mortgage on your homes only assures him that no one tries to keep his Money without paying back the loan. Being of fine character and not inclined to cheat anyone, you agree this is fair. So, loaning each family $100 each at 10% interest for a year, he leaves them to exchange labor and foods with each other using the Medium of Exchange (the Bankers Money) among themselves to circulate as a measure against the Credits and Debits of their exchanges. Now I ask you at year end, when the Banker returns to collect on the loans, will you and your neighbors be able to pay him back?

Well, the answer is Yes, for one family, maybe for a second, and No for sure, for the third family. How do I know? Like the Banker knew right from the start, I know that since only $300 was loaned into circulation ($100 to each family) and at 10% interest, each agreed to return $110 for a total of $330 due the Banker. Therefore, depending on who traded what with whom, and where the debits and credits currently lay, one maybe two could be holding their $110 payment, but the third cannot possibly be. Why, because the $30 of Interest was never created in the first place. So, in order for anyone to be able to pay back their loan, they need to be holding some of the money in circulation that was previously loaned to their neighbors. Their neighbor being without that "Money" cannot possibly pay back more than they even had in the first place.

So, now when the Banker proposes foreclosing on yours or your neighbor's home for failure to pay, will you think of yourself or you neighbor as a deadbeat? A lousy "Money" manager? Or will you recognize the Banker as a conman and a thief? The Banker in our example may not have known which of those he lent the Money to would fail, but he knew for sure, at least one and just as possibly, two, would in fact fail, as sure as the sun coming up tomorrow!

So as the Banker hides out among the millions of daily transactions and those who have managed to get ahead as the lender and provider of opportunities, in fact he is a calculating, scheming, and conniving snake in the grass. In a microcosm, like our example, he would end up tarred and feathered if not hung from a tree. But in the macrocosm of today's society and economy he is hid away, throwing dispersion at those caught in his web.

If you return to the illustration, we used earlier to show how the first person awarded the Printing Press would have noticed that printing too fast would cause a rise in prices due to inflation of the Money Supply, and too slow would cause a reduction of price in non-essential goods due to not enough Money to go around. When you go from spending into circulation, to loaning into circulation, you compound exponentially your control over the expansion and shrinking of the Money Supply.

With Government overspending and easy lending and credit policies you can heat up the economy in no time. More Money means more people spending, having ideas, starting businesses and hiring labor. In other words, you put wealth creation into high gear. With increased taxes and tightened lending policies, Money is siphoned out of the economy like a vacuum. Remember as people and businesses pay back the loans for which the interest was never printed, the supply of Money disappears. This means less spending, layoffs, business reduction and closures. This all means defaults and the Title of all property reverting to the Bankers to sell over again in the next expansion.

In the current system, if new Money, to fill the need of a Medium of Exchange and to provide for a place to get a hold of the interest for previously lent Money, did not continue to be printed all Money in circulation would disappear. Because of those paying off old loans with Interest and nothing new being added, all Money would vanish; leaving only those remaining defaulters unable to pay.

Because of this catch 22 that the Bankers, along with our ignorance and apathy, have created, this situation of crime, corruption, poverty and economic slavery, will be almost impossible to end prior to worldwide economic collapse, destruction and widespread suffering for almost all. Certainly few, if any, politicians will promote change or ever admit to the root of our problems, knowing few in the populace will be willing to submit to the sacrifices and hardships necessary to bring about change for the next generation. Unfortunately, not doing so will be even worse.

CHAPTER 2

Dejure vs Fiat

Hopefully, the previous Chapter has delineated a clear difference between "Dejure" (Lawful Money) and its "Fiat" (Arbitrarily decreed Money) replacement. I think it is reasonable to presume most people, given a choice, would prefer to exchange their valuable time, labor and property only for an equivalent value in time, labor or property in return. The fact that most people do otherwise today is more a matter of misunderstanding and a lack of choice than it is a willingness or intention to accept less. For many centuries gold, silver and other precious metals and stones have been used and accepted as a Medium of Exchange. Not only between individuals, but between nations. These items have been used because they fit the attributes of a proper medium. Not only are they durable and recognizable but they are almost universally desired for many purposes beyond being just a Medium of Exchange, and therefore make for a good store of value as well. Add to this that their release from the earth requires as much time, labor and effort as many of the items they are exchanged for.

Imagine centuries ago, leaving the Middle East and spending many weeks traveling over to India to purchase spices and precious goods to sell. When you arrive with your "Middle Eastern Bucks", very pretty pieces of paper, no one there will sell anything to you. They have no idea what they could use them for. When you explain that everyone back home accepts them, they laugh, and say "well not here". They might explain to you that they would accept some figs, dates or olives in exchange for their spices but certainly not this paper. You might say the trip was too long and hard, and that those items might have spoiled. They would ask then, if you have gold or silver or knives or swords, maybe even ask for your camel, but the last thing they want is pieces of paper with your Sheikh's picture on it. I am sure you get the point.

Even Paper Money itself came on the scene not as a Medium of Exchange or as Money, but rather as a receipt for actual Money. As Gold Certificates and Silver Certificates these Receipts could be redeemed for the actual gold or silver quantity that the paper Receipt designated.

It soon became apparent that the people would use the paper just as readily if there was not a vault of gold to go to. In 1933, FDR began fiddling with gold reserve requirements. He suspended the gold standard except for foreign exchange, revoked it as the universal legal tender for debts, and banned private ownership of significant amounts of gold coins. These were all partial measures that set the trend in motion for separating our currency from gold. The final move to turn the US dollar into a complete fiat currency was made by President Nixon in

1971 when he canceled the direct convertibility of the US dollar into gold.

As you can see the Powers that be took advantage of the majority's propensity to continuously exchange the Receipts of gold and silver rather than the gold and silver itself. So, does this prove the Paper Money to be as good a Medium of Exchange as gold and silver? Certainly not! So long as the maker of the Receipt had to be prepared for the eventuality of delivering gold and silver in exchange for the Receipt's return, he was held liable to the Law and circumstances of his failure. But with the changing of the Receipt into a simple Promise to Pay Nothing except another paper Promise to Pay Nothing the evil powers previously described regarding Paper Money were unleashed.

The people having been made accustomed to the exchange of the Receipts for goods denominated in this many or that many dollars saw little change in their habit of exchanging goods and labor for Paper. Especially since the Paper Money looked almost identical to the Gold and Silver Certificates except now, they were not redeemable Certificates but Federal Reserve Notes. These redeemable only in other Federal Reserve Notes. But since few ever redeemed them anyway and even fewer understood that Federal Reserve was not our government it wasn't long before the Dollar, a precise measure of gold, became known as a piece of paper with a one printed on it.

Before exploring more of the nuances and circumstances created by this Game of Monopoly, we have all been dragged into with Paper Money, let us look at the principles of the original system without Money.

Like my previous example of being one of the first few settlers here in the New World, a system without a specific Medium of Exchange would have had most people supplying themselves with all the necessities of life. This could only be accomplished by spreading out on the land and laboring long and hard. In fact, without the right to property and land, life, let alone freedom would be impossible. Although we are born today into a world full of material things food, shelter, clothing, cars, buildings, computers, you name it, they all came first as ideas and concepts. All these ideas have been material-ized out of the ground, literally, including the body we labor with. But that is another story!

In a world without Money, I might take some of the wood I chopped to keep warm and trade it with my neighbor for some of the corn he grew to fill his stomach. This would be a benefit to us both. Rather than me being warm but hungry and him being full but cold we are each made warm and full by this exchange. Today such an exchange is called "Bartering". Without so-called "Money" "Bartering" would probably be the system of exchange. This system works fine between neighbors in close proximity to each other and up to a certain number of participants. But as the number of participants in-crease and the distance between them widen, keeping track of what is due who and when would become difficult.

After some time, I would get tired of receiving only corn for my wood and then trying to get someone I didn't provide wood to directly to take some of my neighbor's corn in exchange for what I wanted from them. It would become cumbersome quickly. At some point this would lead to some commodity largely accepted by most to become used as the place holder of value until it could be moved on in exchange for another particular need or want. This tendency toward a non-perishable, durable, easily recognized and desired Intrinsically Valued Commodity, such as gold and silver becomes natural. In places where these have been unavailable such as prisons, the commodity of choice may be cigarettes, stamps or packages of Mackerel or other food stuffs. But no matter where or what society, the tendency of a Medium of Exchange to develop is almost inevitable. Unlike Paper Money the parties to Bartering are usually satisfied, both coming away from the deal considering themselves each to be in a more satisfactory position than before the exchange.

Since the time, effort and availability of producing one set of items is exchanged against those same consid-erations in another set of items an inherent fairness prevails. It Prevents one person getting ahead of his neighbor by virtue of the other somehow having to lost out, a feature prevalent in Paper Money. Variations in the wealth of the majority occurring largely due to willing-ness to labor and ingenuity rather than the timing of money manipulations and position within the scheme.

The Price of an item in the Barter Exchange Market, the real Free Market, whether measured in bushels of corn or ounces of silver, is determined by the Principle of

29

Supply and Demand. The availability of an item, its Supply, and the desirability, its Demand, Governs its Market Price. Given a steady Supply and equally steady Demand for a particular item its Price should remain the same (stable). This due to its relative position with those commodities or Medium of Exchange being used to purchase or exchange for it. In a just system the Money itself should not have a bearing on the Price of the item sought. Supply and Demand will have an effect. If for instance a poor or damaged crop of corn occurs yet just as many people want to obtain corn as last season the fact that there is less of it to go around (meet the demand), will cause the Price to go up because the Demand remains. The Free Market's inherent adjustment to this circumstance is for Prices to rise to a point at which enough people will prefer not to pay such a high price any longer and change their habit or the amount of corn they eat for wheat or some other alternative or do without. At this point the Price will stabilize, Demand again being just enough.

Conversely, should an unusually abundant crop of corn occur and there becomes such a large amount of corn with no more demand for it than its previous season the opposite will occur. Prices will drop until a point is reached where more people decide on corn rather than some alternative, finally again stabilizing the Price as enough Demand arrives to meet Supply.

In this way the Free Market is self-governing. If after an extended period of high Prices the desire for said good or service remains high, more producers or service providers will begin to see the availability of opportunity and direct their efforts towards producing and providing for that Demand. The addition of more producers or service providers will cause the Demand on any one source to go down thereby meeting the Demand which in turn will cause Prices to stabilize or reduce due to the new increased Supply.

Conversely Market adjustment for over Supply or too many providers will be to see Prices drop for that commodity or service to a point where the producer cannot meet the actual cost of providing the good or service and will therefore refrain from producing or serving until a stable level is reached.

A truly Free Market a market not manipulated by government, organized crime or Money Suppliers is a self-regulating market. Inflation and Deflation do not occur therefore neither do recession, depression and bubble markets.

Are you thinking I just explained how Prices can go up and down in a Free Market so how can I say there is no inflation or Deflation? Far too many Economists have taught students for years that the definition of Inflation is Rising Prices, and that Deflation is Declining Prices.

Unfortunately, our Public School System is not de-signed to promote learning how to learn and critical thinking. Instead of teaching students how to learn, think and research they teach instead "What to know". By teaching so-called facts and giving students lists of things to memorize they program them to accept whatever they are told. Students are rewarded with high test scores when they parrot the information taught to them and punished with low scores, lack of acceptance and advancement, when they do not receive the material correctly. With such a system when error is introduced it is perpetuated for way too long by way too many.

The problem with too many Economic Books and Classrooms is that they try to analyze all the factors of Supply and Demand and the interaction between firms, households and government but leave out the option of variations in the Money System. Taking for granted that Money is some understood constant. That Government must regulate and intercede in the Market is an unquestioned premise from which they proceed.

As proof of these false presumptions, they inevitably bring up the infamous German runaway inflation of the early 1920's and the U.S. Stock Market Crash of 1929 and the ensuing Great Depression. By describing the horrible effects of each of these events on the Market and Society they conclude that the Free Market obviously cannot self-regulate. Without ever analyzing the Money System and situation at that time they explain why Government from then on has discovered it must have a hand in the regulation and management of the economy.

The fact, however, is that each of their examples presume it was a Free Market in place in Germany and in the U.S. at the time. But there is nothing free about a Market when a small group is in control of a Fiat Paper Money Medium of Exchange. These events have long been proved manipulations of the Money handlers at that time, yet schools continue to teach economics based on these false premises.

Think logically, at the time of the Great Depression did America suddenly not have the amount of farmland it had a few years before? Did it suddenly have less people willing to work hard for their families? Did our vast natural resources suddenly dry up? No! Every one of these things still existed. So, what happened? How did we go from boom to bust and soup lines?

Well sixteen years after giving away the People's Printing Press (the right & responsibility of Congress to coin Money and set the value thereof) to the European Bankers they were ready to make their great robbery and Money manipulation. As described in the first Chapter they used the power of this Press to set the People to creating great wealth until they were ready to take Title of it all to themselves; By halting the Press, depressing the Money Supply and plummeting Prices of everything other than the necessities. Despite fertile farmland and plenty of laborers for factories the lack of a sufficient supply of a Medium of Exchange left everyone with the inability to conduct commerce. (Trade)

So, contrary to popular belief, Inflation, is not Rising Prices. Rising prices are an indication that Inflation is occurring. It is a symptom of Inflation but not its cause. Just like a rash around a Bee sting. The rash is a symptom of being stung by a bee. The skin no more decided to rash on its own than a Price decides to rise. Something caused the rash just like something causes Price to rise.

In a Free-Market prices rise and fall and find their equilibrium as previously explained due to Supply and

Demand. The Free Market, if truly free, will find its natural equilibrium much faster than any other system devised by Government or Bankers. It will do so without seriously affecting other unrelated commodity Prices.

Inflation is the increase of the "Medium of Exchange" or "Money Supply" in excess of the creation of new wealth. In other words, more Money chasing the same amount of goods. Or too much Money chasing not enough goods. Whether done steadily over time or done rapidly over a short span Money being introduced into circulation at a rate higher than that of actual wealth creation is Inflation. The difference in the rate and speed of it will only make a difference in how fast the symptoms become visible as Rising Prices.

Conversely Deflation is the decrease in the "Medium of Exchange" or Money below that of actual wealth creation. In other words, not enough Money to purchase the available goods being produced. Whether decreased slowly over time or rapidly a reduction of the Money in circulation below the availability of goods (real wealth) is "Deflation". The difference in the rate and speed of it again determining the speed of which the symptoms become visible as falling Prices, unemployment and recession or depression.

In a true Free Market where the Medium of Exchange used as Money has its own intrinsic value and cost in terms of production and labor, its self-regulating Supply and Demand Equilibrium makes for much less frequent and erratic changes in the equilibrium of those other goods and services being measured by it. Such items as gold and silver historically fitting the bill.

Should a rapid change occur in the Supply and Demand of the commodity being used as Money whether due to war, or a small group seizing control of its production or for any other reason, other non-perishable substitutes will take its place. Other goods already having their equilibrium value would simply be substituted such as so much silver instead of gold or so much brass, copper or other commodity instead of either silver or gold. Just as when Oil Prices become too high people begin heating their homes with natural gas thereby reducing Demand for Oil eventually capping or reducing Oil's Price.

These natural decisions and changes made by the people, the Market participants themselves, are far superior to the illogical, capricious, corrupt favoritism, self-serving dealings and ambitions of politicians and special interests.

To recap, changing Prices in a Free Market occur due to Changes in the circumstances of Supply and Demand. They quickly find a new equilibrium naturally on their own. Changes in Prices in a Controlled, Regulated or Manipulated Market can be from either changes in the circumstances of Supply and Demand, changes in the Supply of Money or a combination of both. This serves to make the causes more difficult to determine and thereby slows or continuously skews the possibility of achieving Market Equilibrium. The attempts to regulate a return to Equilibrium, whether sincere or corrupt, usually serve to unduly enrich some at the expense and damage to many others.

CHAPTER 3

Today's Economy

In the first chapter we examined the questions, "What is Money?" and "What's it for?". It was argued that "Money" is an "Idea" represented by some commodity or material and that it was "For" use as a "Medium of Exchange" to facilitate the exchange of goods and labor within a Society. Further that such facilitation and exchange promoted the welfare of all by increasing wealth and leisure and allowing for the storage of value into the future.

It was then argued that there are better and worse materials that can be used to fit the common attributes desired in a Medium of Exchange. Such things as being durable, recognizable, portable and having intrinsic value. It was shown that numerous items and materials have been used throughout history some meeting the desired attributes better than others. Gold, Silver and other coin-able metals among the most widely accepted.

We saw that "Dejure Money" was a more difficult system to corrupt and manipulate as opposed to that of a "Fiat Paper Money" system. We examined the three main systems or methods of developing a Monetary System. One by having a Medium that itself was one of the commodities and goods that had a value of its own, due to the fact that equally, time and labor was needed for its production, just as the goods it sought after. This Medium rising up within the system along with all the other representations of wealth (Real Goods). The Second system being a Fiat Paper Money having no intrinsic value of its own but being foisted upon society by decree of Government. It entering into circulation as a Medium of Exchange by being spent into society by Government or its creators. The Third system a Fiat Paper Money like the second only exponentially more evil and corrupt entering circulation by being lent into society as opposed to spent in.

We examined the effects of Supply and Demand on the Price of goods under each system. It was shown how the circumstances of Supply and Demand had an effect on Price within a true Free Market but that a new Equilibrium would be quickly arrived at. The lie that Inflation is Rising Prices or that Falling Prices is Deflation was exposed. It became clear that those symptoms of Inflation and Deflation are caused by deliberate manipulation of the Money Supply. It was shown how this corruption is compounded with the addition of Fractional Reserve Banking and Interest (usury).

It should be made clear here that the "Truly Free Market" to which I refer in these examples no longer exists if ever it did. Although some individual Markets or segments of the overall Market may be more free than others, no Market today is truly a Free Market. All countries today are either fully controlled or seriously affected by the Monopoly on the "Medium of Exchange" (everyone's Money) held by the International Bankers. This Monopoly run in the fashion of the Third and most corrupt system that I have described. The laws, politicians, and world leaders all largely controlled and or put in place at the behest and purchase of these Money Men. Even those few nations who have held out against them are seriously affected by them and are constantly under threat of attack and takeover from within and without. These holdouts having their own selfish systems far from being Free Markets are dwindling in number quickly. Such countries as Iraq, Afghanistan, Libya, Yemen, and North Korea.

Whether claiming the ideologies of Capitalism, Communism or Socialism today's ideologically amalgamated democracies are all under this system of economic slavery. Those third world countries undergoing the development of their natural resources and labor forces with development loans from the World Bank and International Monetary Fund (IMF) will soon have their countries stolen and people enslaved by the same Powers that be.

Even the so-called "Black Market" which some have called the only Free Market is not actually a Free Market either as the risks inherent with being involved with it cause wide and varied Price, Supply, and Demand problems. Case in point the vast accumulations of wealth by drug lords who control the Supply and Prices of substances that would otherwise only bring them pennies. Additional ramifications exist when using the

Bankers "Money" in a Market outside their system of Tribute (taxes). Therefore, whether or not in direct control the dominance of their system affects every other. If there is no Truly Free Market, then we appear to be at the mercy of Controlled Markets. As we have seen, that Control, at least the major portion of that Control, is wielded by the owners of the Printing Press Money, the International Banksters. Additional chaos comes from the fact that it is not total control, at least not yet.

Being that the Government of the various Nations are also made up of men, both elected and otherwise, who enjoy like the Bankers, positions of Power and Control as well, they hold onto their own means of enrichment. Just as our Bankers use their control of the so-called "Money" as their means to Power and Riches so the Officials of Government use their control of so-called "Law" for the same ends. And as if the dynamic between these two sometimes cooperative and sometimes opposing Powers were not enough to permanently prevent the economy from ever finding a Free Market Equilibrium, we introduce yet a third Power. This third and possibly largest Power is also the most uncoordinated Power.

The Power of the People's Majority although controlled and herded and milked by the other two, like an elephant tied to a tent peg it could easily pull away if not for its conditioning. The backbone of our industry, the possessor's of trade skills, the fillers of the ranks of our military and an uncontrollable mob if incited are kept from the knowledge and reason for the economic chaos and their lack of freedom. They are used as beasts of burden by the Bankers to create their Wealth, which they use to obtain Power. They are used as horses for the Politicians to ride into Government seats of Power which *they* use to obtain Wealth. In each case they are lied to and stolen from having their own vast Power and possibilities of Wealth taken from them by being divided and conquered. By being divided into Black and White, Rich and Poor, Democrat and Republican, Conservative and Liberal, Men and Women and an endless list of others the ability to unite is sabotaged.

We are controlled by the Bankers, by their manipulation of Prices, the availability of loans, and the supply of Money and Credit. We are controlled by Government and their manipulation of the Law, Taxes, Regulation and Foreign Policies. We control little to nothing having given it up to the other two to take care of us.

It has been shown how the Bankers rob us by their control over the Printing of Paper Money. By expanding and contracting the Supply of Money in the economy. With Fractional Reserve Banking they lend us Money to buy our homes with. Money, they got out of thin air yet with the addition of interest cause us to work 15, 20 and 30 years to pay back almost three times that which was borrowed. Vast amounts of Interest are paid to Banks in order to maintain a so-called "Good Credit Rating". People don't realize they are buying that "Credit Rating" with their time and effort and hard-earned Money. A person of great integrity never having owed anyone or been late in paying on an agreement can have inferior or no credit because of their lack of borrowing and making enough Interest payments. Hence our behavior is controlled by our desire to maintain Credit.

Our behavior is further controlled by their ownership of the now only six or seven Media Conglomerates that bring us 98% of all the news we see. In this fashion we are offered our choice of one of the two acceptable opinions to have on any topic. By funding the huge cost of acquiring a political seat in Government we are offered the great democratic choice between their candidates, yes man one or yes man two.

Our Money choices along with numerous other choices are manipulated not only by the Money Men but by Government. Today Government tentacles have reached into every aspect of our lives from Education to Health Care to the number of gallons to flush our toilets. Through Subsidized Funding, Taxes, and truck loads of Regulations, our behavior is influenced and directed. By Subsidies to some industries and penalties to others, unfair competition is created and fostered, unduly enriching otherwise unprofitable ventures and bankrupting viable ones.

Huge swings in Supply and Demand can be caused, widely affecting the Price of goods both plentiful and scarce. By funding schools in various areas, discrimination is exercised. In others, budgets are driven to heights unsustainable by the community without continued funding, forcing them to participate and add programs and curriculum they would not otherwise agree with, in order to maintain funding. Farmers are paid not to grow crops and others are paid more than a Price the Free

Market would bring them otherwise. Again, causing Supply, Demand, and Price issues that are unforeseen for the consumer. The list of Subsidies and their illogical implementation and consequences could fill numerous books.

Truckloads of Regulations on every conceivable topic and aspect of our lives make every one of us daily violators and criminals (according to them) in more ways than most are even aware of. These violations piling up and waiting in store to be used against the individual who may become the target of any particular agencies need to increase their budget. Or against the individual who may inadvertently exercise free speech or some other Right in his effort to correct a usurping Government agent or official.

Regulations can be used to restrict competition in certain industries. This affects the control of Supply, Demand, and Price for those favored and the budgets and well being of those dependent on that Market. In many cases Government attempts to create jobs and spending in particular industries and areas. By Regulation they cause businesses they deem too profitable to make certain expenditures to other individuals, areas, or industries that they want to enhance. For instance, by regulating a requirement for certain insurance, safety equipment, or disposal methods. Not all Regulation is done with bad motives in mind, but all Regulations have consequences favored by some and opposed by others. All, however, have costs which affect the Markets and are paid for by the people. Whether Taxes or Regulation, all businesses pass costs along to the consumer.

Taxes contrary to most people's understanding do not serve to run and sustain our government. Most believe a portion of everyone's Income is taken and pooled together to pay for Government to exist. This is a naive concept that is promoted by Government and the Money Men alike so that they can elicit the aid of those indignant citizens who pride themselves on paying their "Fair Share". This "Sour Grapes" attitude helps discourage and discover so-called "Tax Cheats" and evaders. The Warren Commission during Ronald Reagan's Presidency found those "Income Taxes" we think run Government are gone before covering the cost of their collection and payment of Interest on the Debt is met.

The majority of American Families today with Incomes below $50,000 who have dependent children do not even pay "Income Tax" and in most cases receive "Transfer Payments" in the form of "Earned Income Credit". In other words, they get back a check from the Government for Money they never even paid into it. They are receiving Money from the "Income Taxes" of others who did pay. Hence the term "Transfer Tax".

Some reading this are saying, "What do you mean?", "I paid plenty". That "Plenty" that was taken from your check was not "Income Tax" per se but rather Social Security and Medicare and as much as they took from you, they took again from your employer. Or if self-employed you paid double. But none of that is Taxes to run the Government. That is for paying all the people that are retired or disabled. No, it doesn't go to any so-called "Trust Fund" for your retirement years it's just another "Transfer Tax" from you to others. Hopefully when you retire there will be yet others still producing so you can get yours. But there are no guarantees. After all, how can you guarantee a Ponzi Scheme. Some call it the largest one ever but that award goes to the Bankers and the owners of the Money Printing Press.

Despite all that, we all pay more than our fair share of Taxes. Although some may be able to avoid, evade, or pay more or less "Income Taxes" most other Taxes are unavoidable. Sales Taxes, Meal Taxes, Gas Taxes and a long list of others are paid by all regardless of income differences. The most hideous of which is that of Inflation and the shrinking value of our Money. If a particular item can be bought for $10 this year and the same item (no more or less supplied or demanded) next year costs $12 then you have paid a $2 hidden Tax or loss in purchasing power.

This is why saving Money in an inflationary period is foolish. Because next year it will not be able to purchase what it can today. In a period of inflation, the saver is penalized while the person who lives above his means on credit is rewarded. For example, two men go out to look at Big Screen TV's at $2,000 one decides to put away savings each month for a year when he plans to come back and buy it. The second decides he must have it now and charges it. Next year after saving $2,000 the first comes back to find the TV is now $2,400 while the second is paying his $2,000 TV off with dollars that are now worth less and has enjoyed the TV for a year. In periods of Deflation on the other hand the advantage to each is reversed.

Taxes are used by certain agencies to increase their budgets. Taxes for the most part, however, are to control behavior and to act as a secondary control valve against Inflation and Deflation. By increasing Taxes demand for goods and expansion of industry can be dampened and the excess "Medium of Exchange" (Money) can be siphoned out of circulation. A reduction in Taxation can have the opposite effect.

By giving Tax Breaks to some and Hikes to others behavior can be controlled and directed toward certain activities. Favorable Tax Rates for married couples over singles and dependent children Tax Credits can promote marriage and childbirth. Just as high Taxes for gas and Credits for solar or windmills can promote the changeover to alternative energy sources. Tax breaks and incentives on Real Estate causes savings and investment toward new building of home and apartments to accommodate population growth. By applying this idea to certain industries or geographical locations they can cause the development of one location in favor of others. The continuous compounding of these powers and temptations by these controlling Social Engineers and experimenters, looking to craft the Utopian Society of their dreams, have reeked much havoc in the lives of our families and the structures of our institutions societal, industrial, governmental and ecclesiastical alike.

The one thing that should be remembered regarding Taxes is that only we the people pay them. Only individuals pay Taxes! Governments, Corporations and other institutions do not pay Taxes. Individuals will only willingly and knowingly accept a certain amount of individual tax burdens before becoming extremely agitated and begin to change over their political choices for others. That is why Politicians will demand the Rich pay more and suggest raising Corporate Taxes etc.. These are just collectivist methods of hiding a greater tax burden. Corporations and all for profit businesses exist and function to create a profit. *ALL* Taxes and expenses including the cost of Regulation is and has to be passed on to the consumer in the Price of the goods and services they pay for. If this in not done the business will not profit and therefore not continue. Therefore a 50% Tax Rate whether the individual is seen to pay 10% and the business 40% is nonetheless equal to the individual paying the whole 50%. The only difference being how much is called Tax and how much is called Price.

The old saying too many cooks spoil the pot certainly has its application when applied to the current economy and the divided interests of those manning the various control levers. It should be coming clearer as to why Market Equilibrium cannot be achieved in a corrupt, controlled or manipulated Market.

CHAPTER 4

Appreciation & Depreciation

The size and scope of the problems created by this corrupt system and our would-be Puppet Masters must seem too overwhelming for any individual to think they can make a difference. The fact that our Country may still be freer and offer a better life for more than those in many other Countries should not be an excuse to accept corruption, be apathetic or bury our heads in the sand. Conversely the Power of the Majority throwing off one bad system ignorantly for another is not a solution to the problem either.

Knowledge and understanding of sound Money Principles must be increased among the populace to prevent one demagogue after another pulling and dividing the people into un-united splinter groups.

There will always be varied interests and opinions among various families, groups, and institutions that make up a society and Country and most especially one consisting of multiple races, cultural traditions, and religious persuasions. If a basic core set of values and principles however are not held up above all the other dividing factors by a large majority, no Country or Society can long endure.

America more than any other nation on earth is comprised of people originally from every other Country in the world and made up of diverse races, ethnic traditions, and religious beliefs but largely in all stages until most recently the overriding Principles held by everyone of the various peoples who made their way here did so because of the Principles they heard that America stood for. Mainly those embodied in our Bill of Rights and the Declaration of Independence. Those of Freedom of Speech, Freedom of Religion, Innocent Until Proven Guilty, Law and Justice for All, Equality in the basic value of Human Life.

All these things today are slipping away from us because we have let demagogic politicians, bought and paid for by the Money Men, lead us all into our divided splinter groups each looking to get ahead (of others) by shifting our focus from Principles shared by all to those of our own immediate needs and wants.

Anyone who has ever served in our Military have raised their right hand and sworn an oath to uphold and fight for our Country and its Constitution against all enemies both Foreign and Domestic. Politicians are always sending us to war and pointing out our Foreign enemies but no one ever seems to point out the Domestic enemy. Those traitorous individuals and groups that have entrenched themselves in positions of Power within our own Government. Who daily work to undermine the Constitution and our Rights. Who continuously allow us to be plundered by a Fiat Money System they dare not mention.

Up until this point I have tried to give a basic understanding about Money. What it is and Why a Medium of Exchange is necessary to facilitate trade, a division of labor and to bring about leisure. More importantly I have tried to emphasis the importance of using a proper Medium with a proper Method of introducing it into circulation. In fact, I have attempted to show that those choices are so important that they can make the difference between Freedom and Slavery. I have attempted to express that this is not just one of many political issues but a core issue underlying all other issues in society.

It is not my intention to bring discouragement or despair nor admit defeat to a hopeless cause; But rather to overcome apathy and procrastination. It is my intention to raise awareness and bring understanding and to eventually outline the Principles needed and the steps necessary to bring a true Free Market System for the benefit of all people.

Before I make a case for remedies, however, let us look at a few more of the terms, issues and nuances of the systems we are currently forced to participate in. Just like the game of Monopoly the better we know the rules, reasons, and options the better we are likely to do.

Unlike the game of Monopoly, which we can just forgo playing if we don't like it, life must be participated in unless we are willing to forgo it altogether and no longer live. Food, shelter, and clothing are the necessities of all. As previously shown without the cooperation of others the adequate acquisition of those necessities would require most of every hour not spent on sleep. As discussed previously Barter and then a Medium of Exchange (Money) allow for the specialization of labor, time and talent which in turn reduces the time and effort of all needed to be spent to acquire life's necessities.

With the division of labor brought about by a Medium of Exchange time previously used in the production of necessities may now be used elsewhere. Some might exert effort into the production of non-necessities or items of convenience that become desired and used by others in their hours of leisure. This further increases the wealth, leisure, and quality of all lives. Although differences in the amount of wealth acquired by some would still exist this would be largely due to the time, effort, the mastering of skills and ingenuity as opposed to the fluctuating value of the Currency, Market Timing or a Favored Position.

First bearing in mind that the above is the basics of the formation of all Markets and second that all Markets if left to their own devices are largely auctions that have developed an Equilibrium. Remember as explained in our discussion of Supply and Demand under each Money System that a Free Market will quickly find its Equilibrium. As an auction Price goes up for an item, that many bidders desire, and as the Price goes up fewer and fewer bidders continue to bid for the item until the highest Price is discovered for which someone will pay. Conversely, an item at the auction that has no bidders will come down in Price until a Price is found that will attract a bid. In this same way the Free Market finds Price levels at which the Price of each commodity evens out its

Supply against the Demand. After this occurs it no longer has the appearance of an auction because Prices remain level or stable so long as the circumstances of Supply and Demand remain relatively constant.

With these things in mind let us look at the concepts of "Appreciation" and "Depreciation". Are these the phenomenon of a Free Market or a Controlled Market? A Dejure Money or a Fiat Money? Or both? "Appreciation" is an increase in value. "Depreciation" is a decrease in value.

In either a Free Market or a Controlled Market an increase in the Demand for and item will cause its Price to rise and a decrease in Demand will cause its Price to decline. In both Market types the increase in Demand could be from many factors. For instance, with crops such as Oranges an early season frost or freeze could damage the crop or even the trees reducing the availability of Oranges for the Marketplace. So previously where $1.00 was the Price that would put a glass of OJ on the breakfast table of everyone wanting one now with less Oranges $2.00 may be required to sufficiently lower Demand to a point where no more Oranges than are available are Demanded. In this case all those who still had Oranges or containers of Orange Juice that only cost them $1.00 when they acquired it and can now turn around and receive $2.00 would be said to have gained because of the rise in the value of an Orange. This would be "Appreciation" an increase in value.

Conversely if the next season saw no frost and California had a great crop at the same time as Florida suddenly there would be more Oranges and Orange Juice to go around than was actually being Demanded at the $2.00 Price level. Therefore, Prices would fall again until there was enough Demand to use up all the Oranges and OJ available to the Market. If this facilitated a drop in Price from $2.00 back to $1.00 all those holding, Oranges bought at the $2.00 Price level would be said to have experienced "Depreciation": a decrease in value.

There are many reasons why the circumstances of Supply and Demand might change hence equally as many reasons for Appreciation or Depreciation. An increase in Supply or a decrease in Demand will cause Prices to fall vice versa a decrease in Supply or an increase in Demand will cause Prices to rise.

Appreciation or Depreciation is measured from the standpoint of the holder of a commodity or item from one point to the other. As stated above if you hold an item that cost you $1.00 and can now exchange it and receive $2.00, then you have experienced Appreciation of your item. If, however you hold an item that cost you $2.00 and can only now get $1.00 you have experienced Depreciation.

Some reasons for a change in the circumstances of Supply and Demand might include a product or item becoming less desirable because of the invention of a more convenient product. Or the discovery of additional sources of a once rare commodity. A new technology may increase the speed of production thereby making the product much more abundant. On the other side of the coin a once plentiful commodity or resource may now be dwindling causing the little remaining to become much more valuable. Depending on your position with regard to a particular commodity when such a change occurs dictates what you will experience. Holders of the commodity will experience either Appreciation or Depreciation and seekers of it will see higher or lower Prices.

The effects of changes in the circumstances of Supply and Demand, and depending on your position at the time, your experience of Appreciation or Depreciation are equally valid and real no matter the Market type. Whether Free or Controlled all other factors being equal the effects are similar. In a Controlled Market however, the appearance of Appreciation or Depreciation can also be illusory. It can be the imaginary effect of manipulation or more confusingly a combination of both.

With the real causes already shown let us look separately at the illusionary causes. Remember that in a truly Free Market with a Medium of Exchange that has a real value and measure, such as an ounce of silver; Price changes are only due to actual changes in the circumstances of Supply and Demand. This Price change causing the experience of Appreciation or Depreciation for some. But Inflation and Deflation are non-existent. Inflation and Deflation being already shown to be the phenomenon of a Controlled and Manipulated Market. Specifically, an effect of increasing or decreasing the Supply of Money in circulation.

If it is a lie that Inflation is Rising Prices, and I believe that has been clearly demonstrated, then it is equally a lie that you have experienced Appreciation when holding an item obtained when it was $1.00 and is now $2.00 due to a Price increase caused by Inflation. Nor have you experienced Depreciation when the Price falls from $2.00 due to a Price decrease caused by Deflation the effect of restricting the Supply of Money in circulation.

To clarify if we have the production of 100 items (the Supply) and an equal desire for these items (the Demand) in an economy with $100.00 in circulation, to use toward that desire, then the Price will find Equilibrium at $1.00 per item. Should the Controller of the Money Supply inject another $100.00 into circulation and there is otherwise no change in the Supply (the $1.00 items) and no change in the Demand (the desire to have the items) $200.00 now in circulation will be chasing the same 100 items causing a change in Price from $1.00 to $2.00. This change in Price having nothing to do with a change in the circumstances of Supply and Demand but only in the fact that the increase in the Supply of Money is out pacing the production of goods. In other words, because of Inflation.

Has the item become more or less valuable? No! Increased in Supply? No! Increased in Demand? No, but only because the Price was increased to prevent more Demand than items produced. If the Price had remained $1.00 after more Money was pumped into circulation then those desiring that item would increase. Or it may cause the first people who stepped up to buy the item to each buy two leaving a shortage for all the others who would also be willing to pay $1.00 for an item; now that they have $2.00 they could put toward it. By the Price moving to $2.00 only the same amount as before that are willing to part with their whole $2.00 come for the item thereby once again equalizing Supply with Demand.

So, with no real change in Value, Supply or Demand did those who were holding an item that cost them $1.00 experience Appreciation when Price went to $2.00 because of Inflation? No, because they will need that same $2.00 to buy another item. Their actual real wealth has not changed at all. As an example my dad bought a home for our family in 1969 and paid $18,000 as the purchase Price. In 1979 he sold that house for $38,000. Most then and today consider such an occurrence to be a Capital Gain the result of the house Appreciating over time. The Capital Gain being the changing of $18,000 (the Capital) used to make the initial purchase, into $38,000 (the sale Price) the $20,000 increase (Appreciation) being the gain.

But in the very inflationary period of that time is this really what occurred? Or is that what we have been conditioned to believe? Have you ever known a home to Appreciate? I know many will say, "Yes I have had great Capital Gains from Real Estate", and for some in the business of Real Estate Investing that may be somewhat true comparatively but for other reasons. However, for most who buy for the sake of having a home I would argue otherwise.

Homes do not Appreciate. If you doubt that then go buy one for any amount and let it sit there do nothing and see what happens. It will not Appreciate, actually it will deteriorate. It will grow old and fall apart in front of your eyes given time. Without continued maintenance, upkeep and renovation a home will not maintain the value you paid for it. The only thing that leads you to believe otherwise is that Inflation and devaluation of Money (the loss of its purchasing power) causes the number or quantity of Paper Dollars required to be exchanged for that same item to go up in number.

If we return to the example of my dad's so-called "Gain" and consider that of the $20,000 on the home he bought for $18,000 and sold for $38,000 and consider that he paid interest on a mortgage for those 10 years and also poured countless hours of labor painting, papering and fixing it that Gain begins to diminish rapidly.

When adding the dollar costs of these repairs and maintenance to his labor along with the virtual rent of Property Taxes if any Gain remains it is minimal. The real exposing factor comes when you properly consider that he put his family in a home in 1969 for $18,000 and now after selling the first home he still needs a home for his family but it now costs $45,000. So even if we are willing to ignore all the costs of remaining in the previous home and buy the line about the $20,000 Gain from Appreciation an additional $7,000 must be spent or mortgaged to now put the family back in a home.

Over the years these numbers have significantly increased in most areas but the Principle remains the same. If you buy a home for $100,000 and sell it for $200,000, have you really gained if the whole $200,000 is now required to buy the same home you previously paid $100,000 for? The home is no more or less needed or valuable to you now than it was then. When you consider that the interest on the mortgage, the property taxes and upkeep all require your hard earned and labored for Money and that the so-called "Appreciation" you receive in exchange is an illusion created by Fiat Money you are lucky if you are not in the loss column in real terms. After being fooled into calling this scenario a Capital Gain the IRS gives us the privilege of paying taxes on our so-called "Gains".

Let's take two so-called "Investors" today investor one takes his $100,000 and buys a piece of Real Estate with it. Investor two takes $100,000 and puts it in a Money Market Fund averaging 5% interest. Three years later they compare notes investor two's Money Market Account is worth $116,000 and Investor one is proud to declare himself the winner having sold the Real Estate for $125,000. Investor two however says, "Not so fast. What about property taxes, maintenance and insurance?" After computing annual costs for insurance at $600 and taxes at $1,200 and being lucky enough to have no major repairs his cost estimate is $6,000. So, after subtracting that from the $125,000 he has a net of $119,000, still considering himself the better off. After the additional deduction by each for the privilege of paying their "Fair Share" in Capital Gains Taxes are either of them actually in the plus column? When you consider that in real wealth the home that cost $100,000 three years ago now has a Price of $125,000 you can see that after each of their so-called "Gains" that neither of them could purchase back that same home now, yet three years previous they both could have. So where is the "Gain" of these so-called "Investments"? Why are we paying taxes on gains that are not real? Oh! The wonder of owning your own Money Printing Press! Wouldn't it be great! So, as you can see the best of us at handling Money and Investing cannot pride themselves on anything more than managing to be ripped off (stolen from) less than the rest of the people.

This phantom Appreciation and Depreciation created by manipulation of the Money Supply is used by the Bankers to further mystify the causes of the economic chaos and to cloak their larceny. Government uses Appreciation to collect taxes on gains that are non-existent and Depreciation to give tax breaks to certain market sectors to steer behavior. For instance, to aid in the continuation of building, necessary to increase Capital Investment, for additional housing for the population.

Depreciation within our tax code is an allowance for the amounts of "Capital Expenditures" to be expensed out over time. "Capital Expenditures" are the Assets of Business such as buildings, homes, vehicles, machinery and other costly equipment and costs necessary to conducting business. The purchase of the "Capital Expenditures" are not allowed to be deducted fully from the Income of the businesses in the year of their purchase but must be spread out over several years. Schedules of the time allotments of such items are issued by the Tax Man and vary according to class and type of Capital Expenditure. For instance, a truck necessary to conduct business for some company if purchased this year for $20,000 would be allowed to expense out (deduct from Income) only $4,000 for the year and would be allowed to expenses out another $4,000 the following years for a total of five years. The listed schedule for Depreciation of that type of Asset. This time period assumed to be the useful life of the asset before deterioration and need for replacement.

When used in Real Estate this schedule is 27 years for residential and 38 for commercial. Land itself is not depreciable. Although individuals are not allowed this luxury for their homes, I guess they felt they had to be more realistic with Real Estate Investors and admit that homes do not actually Appreciate, but in fact deteriorate without continued investment, so allowing Depreciation as an expense was necessary. Without it continued investment in housing would cease. But as shown in the previous example of the two investors, what most refer to as successful investing and getting ahead is merely not being ripped off (stolen from) like the rest of the people. So, what is counted as great success is simply the feeling and experience all would have if not for Fiat Money.

As an example, if an investor or a group of investors pool together Capital of say $270,000 for the purchase of a Residential Income Property they will receive an allowable Depreciation Expense Deduction of $10,000 each year for 27 years. If we assume they rent this property out for $2,000 per month their income on the property will be $24,000 for the year. From this $24,000 let's assume they pay $2,500 in property tax, $800 for insurance, $200 for town water and average about $1,000 in maintenance costs per year. These total $4,500 and are expenses deductible from the $24,000 Income. This leaves Income of $19,500 but with the allowable Depreciation Expense of $10,000 the taxable Income is reduced further to $9,500. If for the sake of round numbers, we assume these exact numbers for the entire 27-year Depreciation period of this Asset a total of $648,000 would be paid by the renters. At $9,500 per year taxable Income, $256,500 of Income would be taxed. So, $648,000 collected minus the $256,500 taxable portion leaves the investors $391,500 as the non-taxed portion. From this the investors are due their initial Capital Investment of $270,000 used to originally purchase the Real Estate that has now been Depreciated and deteriorated over the 27 years and is now considered worthless (for tax purposes). So, $391,500 minus $270,000 (Initial Investment), leaves the $121,500 amount spent to cover expenses. If we deduct the actual tax from the $256,500 Income portion that was taxable, we can then determine the return on investment remaining. The tax would likely be around 25% the average Capital Gain Tax over the years. So, $256,500 minus 25% or $64,125, leaves $192,375 profit the total investment return after tax and return of Capital.

In other words, $648,000 was collected in rents form an Asset with a useful life of 27 years. If you deduct the price of buying the Asset in the first place ($270,000) you are left with $378,000 from which the actual $4,500 per year of expenses were paid ($121,500) leaving $256,500 taxable Income the average tax on which would subtract from that $64,125 leaving $192,375 as the return on investing in that Asset over that period of time. In simple terms this is a 71% return on the $270,000 over 27 years. Annually less than 3% return on Capital, a figure unacceptable to most investors except most recently with interest rates on savings at nearly zero. A question worth asking is would the profit of $192,375 added to the original Capital of $270,000, a total of $462,375 be enough 27 years later to purchase another piece of Real Estate comparable to that of the original in its day, now? If the answer is yes, then the investor may have profited or at least kept his Money from being worth less. If, however, the answer is no then the investor's so-called profit he was taxed on is actually a loss in real terms.

Now this is not to disparage Real Estate Investment it is only to show the menace and corruption of Fiat Paper Money! In fact, Real Estate Investment over the years has been one of the few and most reliable ways of preventing the loss of purchasing power. Many savvy investors have even managed to profit in real terms. For instance, in the scenario just described most of the $270,000 purchase price would have been borrowed from Banks leaving the actual invested Capital of the Investor to be much less, possibly as little as ten percent of that figure or $27,000. This would increase deductible expenses on the property by the amount of the interest being paid to the Bank and consequently reduce the amount of taxes because of added expenses. In the real world although Depreciation was lowering the value of the house to zero eventually on paper, the maintenance and upkeep along with phantom Appreciation, due to Inflation, would leave the property a much higher sale price at the end of term. Although an additional tax would be due against the sales price of the property the after-tax proceeds would be added to the return on the investment.

So, for example if we take the previous scenario as stated and consider that the investors only put up $27,000 of their own Money and that payments to the Bank come out to around 16,800 annually, that added to the actual $4,500 costs would equal $21,300. With rents of $24,000 that would leave only $2,700 a year profit. On paper however, with $10,000 annual Depreciation Expense allowable they would claim a loss of $7,300. The loss only occurring on paper as the actual rents are covering all the actual costs. This paper loss however would allow the investor to reduce other profits from elsewhere by the $7,300 credit on this investment. Additionally, the Income Tax previously associated with this investment becomes non-existent due to the added expenses of borrowing. The property however is maintained and paid for from the rents maintaining an actual resale value despite paper Depreciation. So, as we have often seen the property sells for a Price above that which it was sold for previously despite the passage of time. This due to inflation, phantom Appreciation and loss of purchasing power of the dollar. However, for this example let's say at the end of term the Investor only sells it for the original purchase Price ($270,000).

This has changed the original scenario where the investors Capitalized the Investment with 100% percent their own Money ($270,000) enjoyed claiming a tax loss for years and after tax on the final sale had a return on Investment of 748% percent overall which computes to about 28% percent annually, a figure more than acceptable to most investors.

The relationship between Depreciation and Tax Basis should be understood. A person's Basis in a Capital Investment is the amount Invested or the Original Price. In our example the Investor's paid $270,000 for the Real Estate to start their investment. That means their Basis in the Real Estate Investment was $270,000. If they turned around and sold the property for $300,000, they would pay a tax, not on the $300,000 sales Price but on the $30,000 difference between their Original Price (their Basis) and the new sales Price. This difference of $30,000 being what they profited and therefore taxed on. Had they sold it at $260,000 instead of $300,000 a $10,000 loss would have occurred since their Basis had been at $270,000.

However, when holding and taking tax deductions for Depreciation each year their Basis is lowered by each claim of Depreciation. In our example this was $10,000 each year. So, if the property was sold for the very same price as originally bought for after taking Depreciation for two years a profit of $20,000 would be considered for taxing. Because $10,000 each year for two years was claimed as Depreciation the Basis was lowered by that amount. This caused the property to be seen as having only $250,000 of the Original Capital remaining in the investment at the time of the new sale.

CHAPTER 5

Interest

So far, we have looked at the effect of Supply and Demand on Price under "Dejure" and "Fiat" Money Systems. The real definitions of Inflation and Deflation have been presented and the concept of Appreciation and Depreciation both real and illusory explored. Let us now look at a concept taking for granted by almost all as being a part of any Money System if not a part of the concept of Money itself.

It is presumed to be only natural that those that lend, save or invest Money receive some amount of "Interest" for it and that those who borrow it should pay "Interest" for it. "Interest" is a charge of fee added to the original amount of the thing borrowed or lent. It has another name however that exposes it for the evil that it is. That name being "Usury". "Usury" is the lending of Money with an "Interest" charge for its use.

Once again you probably think I am being a bit extreme when I use words such as "Evil" or "Corrupt". Therefore, let me give the definition of the words by Webster so you can better decide if they indeed fit the various situations in which I have used them thus far. "Evil" is causing or threatening distress or harm it is also the fact or suffering, misfortune and distress and a source of sorrow, distress or calamity. Now for the definition of "Corrupt". "Corrupt" is to make evil, also to be morally degenerate which is characterized by improper conduct.

The taking of "Interest" impoverishes people, perpetuates poverty and works hardship on not only individuals but on communities and nations as well. As previously stated, if you make your neighbor return a loaf and another half loaf when he borrows only one loaf to begin with, you are not lending you are renting. Whether in Barter, Free Market or Controlled Market "Interest" is "Usury and an extortion. It distorts both Dejure and Fiat Money by causing the Medium of Exchange to go from representing values to making it itself wealth and causing the desire for its possession to be more than the desire for true wealth, the things men can use. In other words, the things bought with Money become less desirable than the Money itself. The enormous sums involved in Interest charges alone can and do enslave men and nations, making them pay tribute for the right to live.

Being a part of the "Rat Race", "On the Treadmill" or "Hamster Wheel" are all expressions for the inability of men to feel they can rest or take a break without the fear of falling behind or losing what they have acquired. This fear or more properly recognition of our current situation is born of Fiat Money, Interest and Improper Taxation above all else.

A proper Medium of Exchange in a truly Free Market Economy with the extension of Credit without the multiplication of debt by Interest and Improper Taxation would be considered Utopian in comparison to the chaos and burdens of our current economic servitude.

It has been previously shown how our current Money is lent into circulation as its path of entering our economy for use as a Medium of Exchange. In the example of your neighbor borrowing a loaf of bread I have shown how true lending is to give and receive back what was given. To do otherwise is not lending but renting. By that example if applied to Money we would see that our Money Supply is not only lent to us but in fact rented to us for a fee. That fee is called "Interest".

The problem with the Banker lending (renting) you Money under the current system is that the fee (interest) that he charges you does not exist. If for instance you were a farmer and you went to the Banker and borrowed $100 and he said, "I will lend you $100 but as a fee when you return my $100, I would like you to include a bushel of corn". Although this would still be a fee it would be one you could possibly pay. With a good crop you could return the $100 and also include a bushel of your added wealth that came from good fortune and labor. But in today's system the Banker lends you $100 and asks for his fee to also be in dollars therefore wanting more back from you than he gave you. You are not allowed to Print Money so where will you get this additional amount of Interest for the fee? You think you will sell some of your extra corn, trade or work and receive the amount needed from someone else. But how will the someone else get Money over to you and still be able to pay back his loan?

Remember all Money is currently lent into circulation and therefore it too must be paid back along with a fee (Interest) that does not exist. If all Money is lent in and all that is lent in is paid back all Money disappears from circulation and the fees (interest) is still due the Banker. In an economy of just a few people this becomes easily apparent. But in an economy of hundreds of thousands, millions and billions it becomes almost impossible to notice. But math is math and the truth of the matter unchanged. In our current system the Banker is not only a Money lender (renter) collecting Usury from his customers but an outright thief. The system is rigged and repayment impossible. Not impossible for all but for most. Some people those who get ahead, do so at the expense of all others who don't. These who get ahead (of their neighbors) do so by being better at playing the game, by being in a position of favor or by being one of the con men. Even many losers in the game are convinced they are winners of it by the numerous methods of extending their time of play until loss, far beyond many others. All these circumstances serving to confuse and hide the rigged nature of the process.

Unfortunately, even coming to recognize the evil nature of the system we are under does not necessarily free us from participation in it nor make us better players within it. Although your awareness, understanding and study of its nature will improve your odds of coming out ahead or on top it does not change the fact that those you are ahead of and on top of are your neighbors, brothers and sisters.

As previously pointed out in the discussion on Appreciation and the illusory nature of it, "Interest" can be much the same. Although most look for and attempt to receive the highest possible returns of Interest on their savings and investments in an effort to get ahead or grow their assets, all but the best of investors is lucky to accomplish a preservation of today's purchasing power into the future. In other words, if the Interest Rate I get on the $1,000 I save today will give my $1,000 savings enough added dollars to have it buy just as much as it would today, tomorrow when I spend it, then I have done alright. Although the added dollars are considered a "Gain" by most if the resulting amount cannot purchase more than the amount originally put away is anything really gained?

Interest is measured in most cases as a percentage of the original amount being referred to, usually referred to as the "Principal". With a loan such as a mortgage the Principal is the amount loaned. The Principal is usually required to be paid back along with some % percentage added, the Interest. In an Investment the Principal is the original Capital Investment made. The amount returned to the Investor above the Initial Capital invested is the Interest or the % Percentage Return on Investment. Some Investments offer fixed, or a set amount of Interest based on the Invested Amount while others are based on performance of the Investment. To get the Rate of Return on an Investment one would take the amount they received above their Initial Investment and divide that amount by the Original Investment and then multiply by 100.

This calculation would result in the "Simple Interest" return of that investment. For example, if you invest $2,000 for a period of time and receive back $2,200 then $200 is the added amount (interest) above the Original Investment of $2,000 (the Principal). To get the "Simple Interest" return as a % percentage take the Interest ($200) and divide it by the Original Investment amount ($2,000). So, $200 / $2,000 = 0.1 now multiply that by 100 and you get 10% percent (0.1 x 100) as your Simple Interest Rate.

"Simple Interest" is the additional amount to the Principal amount only. There is also "Compound Interest" which is the amount of additions added not only to the Principal amount but to amounts of Accrued Interest as well. Most investors look for "Compound Interest" on their investments. Remember that the lender of Money that you borrow is also one of those investors and so most loans are paid and computed on "Compound Interest" not "Simple Interest".

For example, if you borrowed $1,000 for three years at a "Simple Interest" rate of 10% percent you would pay back a total of $1,100 at the end of the loan. But most likely a three-year loan would be given at Compound Interest yet quoted to you at the Simple Interest Rate for a single year. Therefore a $1,000 loan at 10% percent per annum would actually calculate out for you to pay back over the three years a total of $1,331 and actual Simple Interest return of 33.1% percent over that same period.

This phenomenon of rapidly increasing returns is known by some as the "Magic of Compound Interest". This because Interest is being collected on not only the

Principal Amount but also on the Accrued Interest. So, the above calculation for the $1,000 loan with Compound Interest means the borrower is paying $100 after one year this figure added to the $1,000 makes the outstanding loan after one year now $1,100 so therefore the second year, he pays interest on this amount at 10% percent this would mean another $110. That added to $1,100 makes the third-year amount of $1,210 to pay 10% percent interest on again for an additional $121 until finally $1,331 in total is paid back.

As you can see "Compound Interest" can work against the borrower very rapidly and make keeping pace with debt very difficult. And from what we have already seen regarding Phantom Appreciation, Inflation and the loss of purchasing power over time the Saver or Investor needs the "Magic of Compound Interest" just to prevent loss of value. The "Rule of 72" is a handy calculation method to remember when Saving or Investing. This Rule is used to calculate the speed at which your Savings or Investment will double given various Rates of Return. By taking the number 72 and dividing it by the Interest Rate you are receiving on your Money it will tell you how long before that Money will double. For example, if you receive 12% percent Interest your Money will double every six years. (72 / 12 = 6) If you receive 8% percent it will double in nine years (72 / 8 = 9).

Since the Saver or Investor needs to be aware of the need to maintain the purchasing power of his Money the "Time Value of Money" needs to be a consideration in long term contracts. That is why you will see cost of living increases in employment contracts and step increases in rental agreements. Some agreements will cite specific increase amounts in dollars or percentages while others may be tied to things like the "Consumer Price Index", "Gross Domestic Product" or some other Interest Indicator or Market Index.

Today an online internet search will net you many handy tools, spreadsheets and formulas for calculating and answering the questions regarding the "Time Value of Money". Mortgage Calculators where known values can be plugged in to return other unknown values. For instance, by plugging in the Principal Loan or Mortgage Amount to be borrowed along with the Annual Percentage Rate to be charged will return the Monthly Payment Amount that will be required. It will also calculate total amounts of both Principal and Interest that will result over time. It can even show the Balance Remaining after any number of payments or time.

Similar calculators can show what your one-time lump sum amount of savings will become after certain periods of time at various Rates of Interest. Another can show what a certain steady Deposit Amount will become over time at different Interest Rates or conversely what a certain Accumulated Amount would pay out monthly as an Annuity and for how long.

These tools are handy for calculating and planning in advance. Knowing how much you will pay in total on a loan. How long it will take to pay off a Credit Card of a certain balance and rate. If you want a certain lump sum by a certain date in the future what amount you will need to put away now. Or how long your savings will last are all convenient formulas for considering your future.

Like with Real Estate and Appreciation certain savvy investors may use Interest or both Interest and Real Estate Appreciation Investments to come out ahead in the game but for the most part average to above average "Joe" is doing good to accomplish maintaining the Purchasing Power of his Savings and avoiding the con of the Money Men. For everyone else, those who pay almost three times the Purchase Price of their homes before receiving clear Title, and those who cannot even afford a home have a continuous battle against Usury Interest. The battle to break away from economic slavery and avoid bankruptcy is an ongoing struggle that should incense those who understand that we are being charged a rent (interest) on our Medium of Exchange (Money), simply for its use as Money. The fact that this Interest is being charged for Paper that cost almost nothing and for Credit that is created out of thin air makes it all the more sinister.

When we realize that we could free ourselves instantly by canceling the Bankers privilege to control the Money Press and demand that Congress do their job of coining our Money and setting the value thereof, as outlined in our Constitution, the fact that we don't should lead us to question our sanity if not our Courage and Moral Integrity.

CHAPTER 6

Credit

Even more sure than conquest of a Nation or people by war is their subjection through the control of their Money Supply. If a drawback can be found to being the owner of the Money Printing Press it would only be in the warped mind of the Printer in that he cannot steal and control the World quickly enough to satisfy himself. He needs to be self-controlled in the pace of his Printing so as to prevent runaway inflation. If he prints too much too quickly the symptoms of this Inflation will show up in rapidly increasing Prices. This could lead to Money previously borrowed from him being paid back to him with exceedingly less value in real goods and services than could otherwise be extracted. Additionally, it comes with increasingly greater unrest and outcry from the people who threaten to dislodge his political puppets with those who may want to tweak his control and adjust the levers of Law and Regulation. Ultimately unrest can also lead to riots, burned cities and ruined assets.

Whether by design or mistake it's hard to say but the Banker has discovered a nuance in the extension of Credit that adds another control lever to the various levers already at his disposal. Where the overprinting of

Paper Money leads to Inflation appearing in Rising Prices and Rising Interest Rates; the extension of "Credit" has the effect of opposing these symptoms. Both Printing Paper Money and Expanding Credit amount to an expansion or addition to Money in Circulation.

If this expansion occurs at a rate greater than the creation of real wealth (goods & services) then Inflation occurs. If done by Printing Paper the fact that more Money is chasing fewer goods begins to appear quickly in Rising Prices and Rising Interest Rates. This occurs because once this abundance of Paper is in the hands of the people this abundant supply of a Medium of Exchange allows people to transact business with each other over and over again. For instance, one person sells his used car and receives Money for it. He then goes out and uses that same Money to buy a boat and some fishing gear, the one who received this Money in turn buys something else. All these transactions are outside the specific control of the Money Printer or the Government. Therefore, other than their gains on the original Printing and lending the other transactions are outside their purview.

Along comes the "Extension of Credit" which also expands the Money Supply but does so without the same effects as increasing physical Medium of Exchange. This expansion does not even cost the price of Paper and Ink it is created out of thin air. The residual transactions outside the Bankers control that occur with adding Paper Money to the circulation are minimized with "Credit Money". Nothing produced or of any value is lent to the borrower yet he pays back both the Principal Loan Amount and Interest on it from his hard earned real goods, labor and time.

The Inflating of "Credit Money" defies its detection in the symptoms of Rising Prices and Interest Rates usually associated with such Inflation. It does this because the repayment of the extended Credit saps the Supply of Money in circulation at more than twice the speed of its counterpart Paper Money. This occurs because with the lending of Paper Money, at least the Principal portion of the loan enters circulation. This allows for many other secondary uncontrolled transactions while Paper is used as a Medium of Exchange within the economy. Then as the loan is repaid this Principal amount along with Interest is eventually pulled back out of circulation.

However, with "Credit Money" not even the Principal amount is added to circulation so there is no addition to the physical Medium of Exchange used in secondary uncontrolled transactions. Then additionally as soon as repayment begins, the Principal, that was never added to circulation, along with the Interest both get pulled from circulation accelerating the speed of Deflation, shrinking of the physical Money Supply.

In other words, despite Inflating the "Credit Money" the circulating Medium of Exchange is Deflated. This causes a stagnating economy due to lack of secondary transactions and artificially keeps Interest Rates low despite wildly increasing debt.

The fact that today's "Money" or "Medium of Exchange" is made up of both a physical and non-physical character, Paper Currencies and Credit Extension, the variations in the manipulations of each lead to many unintended and unforeseen circumstance. When you add the factor of the numerous hands that hold the various control levers, Central Bankers, Government Currency Controllers, Enemy Nations and consumer confidence, spending and saving, it becomes a recipe for disaster that will not be easily avoided.

This huge imbalance between "Credit Money" that is non-tangible and tangible "Paper Money" that at least serves as a Medium of Exchange, so long as faith in it remains, causes a slowdown in the "Velocity of Money". The average number of times a dollar bill changes hands during the year in these secondary transactions, previously described, is called the "Velocity of Money" by economists.

As real wealth creation which comes from increased goods and services diminishes due to the Deflationary effects of a shrinking Medium of Exchange (the physical dollars) the overall Money Supply continues to grow because of "Credit Extension" (also Money). This further exacerbates the problem in numerous ways. One being that every dollar of the physical Medium (Paper Money) used to pay the Principal and Interest payments originally loaned out as Credit further shrinks the physical Money Supply which itself was borrowed. Another is that the limited physical Money Supply leads to greater use of Credit Extension to both pay for those goods and services that are continuing to be produced and to make payments on previous Credit Extensions.

In other words, as people use their paychecks to cover their mortgage payments or rent they then use their Credit Cards to buy food and gas and other items they need. This leads to yet additional wealth being transferred to the Bankers as they extract a fee in the form of Interest for the Credit Card use not only from the Card Holder but also in fees of at least 2 to 3% percent of every transaction from the seller (Merchant).

As the creation of real wealth slows further the Inflationary effects of the expansion of the overall Money Supply, by Credit, leads to increasing Prices for the necessities of life. The Deflationary effects of the physical Medium of Money leads to reduced Prices in non-essentials, business slowdown and closure, unemployment and discontentment of the people who exert political pressure on politicians. They in turn move Government to act and start tinkering with the levers of control that they hold.

Government Programs that enlarge themselves create some jobs, but none associated with good business practices, like covering costs. Additional welfare, unemployment, subsidy programs, loan guarantees to the unqualified and other stimulus programs largely designed to trickle into the economy from their spending and stimulus is just more borrowing of Credit Extension. All these devises enriching some and destroying others. All this leads to more and more people, businesses and industries living on Credit which is a loan against tomorrows anticipated production.

Eventuality all these players, Government, Corporations and the people will reach a point where "Maximum Credit Absorption" will be reached. This point where current use of Credit cannot be expanded further. Where past and current Credit obligations absorb and exceed available Credit Extension.

Remember all Money whether Paper or Credit is currently loaned into circulation. No Money exists in the current system that is not a loan. That means all Money needs to be paid back and just paying it back causes it to be eliminated (disappear). So where does the Interest come from? Nowhere! It doesn't exist. The illusion that it does, comes from the Banker printing more and giving a second and third person a loan also and when you get some of their Money you are able to pay back your loan. The problem is you don't realize that both the second and third person cannot pay back their loans because you used both yours and some of their Money to physically pay back yours. Therefore, if the Banker does not give a fourth and fifth person a loan there will not be Money enough, after you paid yours, for the second or third person to pay theirs. And on and on the Ponzi Scheme goes until it collapses.

In the above example the addition of Credit will sap the Supply of Money used to pay back the previous loans even faster. So, you should now see that the evil system we currently use has a built in doomsday device! The need to extend Credit or Print Money is unending and ever expanding because to stop is to cause it all to disappear and remove the Medium of Exchange from Society. This would be the breakdown of Society.

We all know our ability to even accept more Credit when it surpasses our Income needs to cease. When this occurs only two alternatives will exist. One will be that Government will finally take back its Printing Press from the Banker and then it will either repudiate all debt or Print Money like crazy to pay off its debt in worthless Paper that it decrees "Legal Tender". This will lead to runaway Inflation and be its own disaster. Or choice two would be to institute a Medium of Exchange with real value and eliminate corruption but when have we known Government to do what is right?

In order to have Credit in an honest Money System someone must save Money before it can be lent. That lent Money (Capital) if put together with other Capital or labor to produce real goods and services adds more real wealth to society. From which the original loan (the saver's Capital) can be repaid. Even with a fee that is a fair representation of the advantage the original loan amount provided. No one is unduly enriched by fraud, and everyone involved in the transaction finding a benefit.

An orderly transfer to a "Dejure" intrinsically valued Medium of Exchange needs to occur simultaneously with the naturally vanishing Medium of "Fiat" Paper Money and Credit as it's discontinued. Without the soon dissolution of the corrupt and the introduction of Honest Value doomsday is unavoidable.

CHAPTER 7

Debt

In the previous chapter "Credit" under our current Monetary System was shown to be an additional means of expanding or Inflating the Money Supply. The result of which can be somewhat contradictory to that of Inflating with an actual increase of the Currency itself. The sudden restriction of "Credit" or easy lending having a quick recessionary effect.

A Monetary System with an Intrinsically Valued commodity based Medium of Exchange, such as gold or silver, is a system of wealth creation. Our current system is a "Debt" based system which creates more and more "Debt". We are literally participating in and have chosen a System that increases Debts for all instead of one that increases wealth for all!

You may be proud to have a good "Credit Rating", but the acceptance of "Credit" makes you a "Debtor". A "Creditor" is one who extends "Credit" or one to whom Money is owed. A "Debtor" is one who owes a "Debt". "Debt" is a condition of owing. Therefore, all who use today's Currencies or Credit are "Debtors". Because all Money and Credit is loaned into circulation it is all owed back to its creator lenders the "Creditors" and all who borrow and use it are the "Debtors".

The so-called "U.S. Dollar" is said to be backed by the full faith and credit of the United States of America. But who is the "United States of America"? Supposedly it is "We the People". So therefore if "We the People" borrow our Money we are "Debtors", and it is our "Debt" to pay back. Our full faith and credit have been pledged. Did you pledge yours?

Did you know the Supreme Court has ruled that if you accept and participate in the benefits of something you cannot disavow the obligations inherent in that same thing? So, since you have enjoyed the benefits along with your fellow countrymen of becoming trillions of dollars in debt and trafficking in the debt obligations of others you now have the obligation along with your children, grandchildren and great grandchildren to labor and pay it back!

How is it that you have been trafficking in the Debts of others? At one time the Christian majority in this Country prayed daily for their debts (trespasses) to be forgiven. The common "Our Father" as it is referred to goes on to recite the promise to forgive others in the same way their debts. This precept not only embraced by Christians but by most all major religions of the World. Unfortunately, through apathy and ignorance our prayers have been answered, in the same way we have handled the debts of others.

They have been held, passed on and multiplied by the "Magic of Compound Interest", Paper Money, Credit and a host of other instruments. Instead of demanding to be paid for our time and labor we accept the debts (IOU's) of others despite knowing "Usury" is being applied to those debts. We then go on and prolong and transfer those debts by using them to get the time, labor and things of others rather than paying for those things.

What do I mean? In other words, by accepting IOU's in the form of other people's debts (Paper Money) rather than only excepting real goods, services or "Dejure Money", such as gold and silver, you cause yourself to be without "Real Money" that you can use to purchase and actually pay your debts with. Since you cannot pay your debts you discharge them instead with other Debt Instruments, offsetting your IOU's with the IOU's of others. By using the Interest-Bearing IOU's of others to get ahead of each other you allow the Money Men, the Creditors of all, to get ahead and on top of everyone.

A "Note" is a written promise to pay a debt also called a "Promissory Note". Look at the so-called "Money" in your wallet. They are "Federal Reserve Notes" they are Negotiable Instruments. Promises to pay! Pay what? Unfortunately, today they are promises to pay nothing. If you came and worked for me giving me of your time and labor, would you be happy with an IOU at the end? Would your grocer or car mechanic be happy to be paid by you with an IOU from me? Worse yet when the IOU I gave you previously comes due would you be happy to have me replace it with another IOU due later? What if I make it more tempting by offering you an IOU and a half when you bring it back next time?

Do you think the above is a silly example? Who

would agree to such a thing? We all do, everyday, that is our system, in fact our system is even worse because they do not only give us an IOU they loan us our IOU's and ask for them back with Interest from us.

Cash, checks, mortgages and bonds, Federal, Municipal and Corporate are all Negotiable Instruments somebody's IOU used as Money. When you buy a home your "Promissory Note" is used by the Banker as Money, from you, deposited in his Bank. This Money (your IOU) is used to give "Credit" to the seller of the home who spreads the pieces of your IOU around to serve as his own (IOU's). The Banker having no stake in the transaction charges Interest not only to you on your own IOU but dozens of others through the Magic of his Fractional Reserve Accounting.

This entire absurdity is begun by our United States Treasury issuing Bonds redeemable with Interest to the "Federal Reserve Bankers" so that they can Print an equivalent amount of "Federal Reserve Notes" (our Money). When the Bond (the Peoples Promise to Pay) matures and comes due we owe the Federal Reserve Bankers all the "Money" the Treasury was allowed to Print. But we also owe them Interest on the Bond now, but that amount was never Printed so that means we need to float another Bond to cover the Interest on the last one. Oh, and since the People have all these Federal Reserve Notes in their pockets there are not enough to pay back so we better float a Bond for that too.

What numb-skull thought this up? Why can't the Treasury just Print the same Money they do anyway without us giving the Bankers an IOU for the privilege of receiving nothing from them? Well both President Lincoln and President Kennedy asked that same question. I wonder if they ever got an answer?

In turn the Federal Reserve Bankers sell these Interest-Bearing Bonds (our debt) in their "Open Market Operations" to third parties such as China and Japan. Thereby along with trade deficits increasing our indebtedness to other nations and the Bankers. These nations all with their own version of the Money Game also brought to them by the Bankers. Interest Bearing IOU's on top of multiplying IOU's in exchange for IOU's. Ever increasing Debts for the People, bribes for the traitors and trillions for the Bankers.

We have voluntarily held out our hands and feet to be shackled and having sacrificed the future of our children and grandchildren for today's comforts and the temporary extension of Ponzi Schemes such as Paper Money and Social Security. We sit idly by allowing Politicians and the News Media to point the finger at every cause under the sun for our problems except for the actual cause of them which appears to be completely off limits.

As if the burden of the chains of the Money Men were not enough our ignorance as to the proper role of Government only increases our Debt adding weight to the chains we have fashioned. We pay taxes on paychecks of IOU's that have yet to be collected and on Capital Gains that turn out to actually be losses in purchasing power. We allow taxation to take the Rights, given to us by the Almighty Creator of heaven and earth, and convert them to privileges offered by Government.

The Scriptures declare and the Founding Fathers of this Great Nation acknowledge Property to be a Right. Among that Property is the Property of a man's labor. It should be self-evident to all that a Right cannot be lawfully taxed. For to tax a Right is to eliminate the Right. Because if I can tax a Right even one dollar then at some point, I can tax it two and so on until it ceases to be a Right by virtue of your inability to afford said Right. To tax a man's property is to set the rate at which you will steal all that he has. But how is Government to be funded if they do not tax Property? Just as with Money there is both an honest and dishonest manner for carrying out the task. The application of Property Tax puts the Property owner on a treadmill that he cannot get off.

Should the Property owner at any point be satisfied with that which he has acquired and discontinue the pursuit of more, a Property Tax immediately requires the divesting or sale of some portion of the acquired Property to pay the Tax on the remainder. This continued reduction of Property to pay the tax on itself will eventually consume all the person's Property or force him back onto the treadmill of Property acquisition.

If a person must continually pay for what is his, then it must be acknowledged that it is not actually his. If a man can have nothing of his own, then even the labor he exerts for the things he acquires is not his own because the actual owner(s) direct his labor. A man's labor that is directed by another is a servant. So, decide wisely whom you shall serve.

The power to tax comes from either conquest or by the consent of the governed. One could argue that ultimately, they become one and the same. In America this power is supposedly delegated by the People to their Representatives. But this power assigned by the Principle of Agency is rightly limited by the Power and Rights of the People who extend it.

In other words, I can extend to my representative or my agent the right to do for me anything I have a right to do myself. But I cannot give him authority to do what I have no right to do myself. If I have a right to defend my property, I can allow another to defend it for me. But I have no right to steal your property so neither can I authorize my agent to do it for me. Even if I have ten agents and they are plenty powerful enough to steal your property for me they have no authority to do so, despite their power and ability it remains wrong or unrighteous. If this is true it remains true if I gather several others who also want to steal your property despite our power, we remain without right. Nothing changes this fact even if we label our self a Democracy include you in it and then vote to take your property from you, it is no less stealing than when I sought to do it myself.

Government's exertion of Power beyond that rightly delegated to it by the People and over things outside the realm of its proper function has led to overwhelming Debts for the People, unfathomable riches for a few and economic chaos for all. Its meddling in the Marketplace with foolish edicts from minimum wage to price controls only serve to add numerous reasons on top of the manipulations of the Money Men as to why it is impossible for the Market to find Equilibrium. Uneducated arguments over such programs from both sides along with the opinions of economists paid to muddy the waters of understanding just serve to take the focus off the real culprits.

Frozen wages, increased minimum wages and price controls do nothing but unduly enrich some, impoverish others and cause shortages or gluts and never aid those they claim to. For instance, Minimum Wage appears to aid the person whose Wage is increased but for everyone whose Wage was increased two more are let go or not hired at all. The employer becomes more discriminate about who gets hired needing the added expense to be worthwhile. Additionally, this euphoria for the lucky recipient of the suddenly higher wage lasts only until the additional cost to the end product or service results in yet higher prices making the new Minimum Wage earner no better off than before percentage wise. Maybe even worse off if fewer family members can get work.

Price Controls likewise cap prices at levels that cause demand for the available commodity to rise with no incentive for the producer to produce more which in turn leads to long lines and shortages of the Price Controlled Commodity. The circumstances of Supply and Demand affect the Market in predictable ways, always have and always will, it is the Markets own nature, and no amount of Regulation and Manipulation can change it. These measures only serve to delay equilibrium and unduly enrich some while impoverishing others causing havoc and destruction of value.

You may feel at this point I have sufficiently beaten the dead horse of our current corrupt and manipulated Monetary System. Although it is discouraging and depressing to look and speak frankly about what has been allowed to occur and to think about or glimpse what will be the result of failing to change our direction; it is necessary to identify the culprits and the problem in order to set a proper course.

In the coming chapters I will move onto a more positive view by reviewing together the advantages and attributes of a true Free Market with an Honest Monetary System. A case for proper functions of Government and its funding as well as the steps necessary to transition from the current system to the new. I will also introduce steps you can take as an individual that will benefit your current position even as you await others to become better educated and awake to the urgent need to change our course.

CHAPTER 8

Money of Value

Having sufficiently exposed the evils of Paper Money and its Credit equivalents along with the motives of those who advocate such systems let us return to the material for use as Money that the ancient Markets have always found naturally at the top of the list. Gold and Silver since the earliest of organized society have been the materials of choice to act as a Medium of Exchange and as a store of value.

These materials are not just readily available to print numbers on and certainly are not produced out of thin air. They require locating and mining as well as refining and forging or stamping all of which amount to time, effort and labor weigh-able against the time, effort and labor of the goods and services they seek to purchase.

Although if gathered up and controlled in the hands of a few, manipulation of the Market would still be possible and detrimental to many but could in no way bring about the widespread economic chaos, slavery and disaster of today's system. The use of both Gold and Silver rather than just one or the other further protects against such manipulation. Additionally, the fact that these materials are themselves commodities that rise up within the Marketplace along with all the other items of wealth and production, means they are not lent into the Market and therefore they are not systematically extracted from it. This means they remain in the Market allowed to change hands in multiple transactions repeatedly.

Even today despite there no longer being a Gold Standard for Currencies to be measured against and despite the widespread ignorance regarding Money almost any political or economic upset causes a flight from worthless Paper into Gold and Silver. This flight to quality and value is almost second nature despite the Central Bankers concerted efforts at times to make it appear that these materials will no longer serve that purpose.

The Currency of many Countries has come and gone but Gold and Silver remains today and will tomorrow. A Country devastated by war that previously had Paper Money accepted by all may find it accepted by no one. Poof! Worthless overnight, the holders of it, sore losers. At times Countries in political upheaval have changed their Money rapidly to a new Money requiring conversion from the old to the new by certain deadlines. This often leaves what was previously much, being converted to little. There is no Currency in the World that cannot be bought with Gold and Silver but the same cannot always be said of the reverse. If a Country were to change their Green Paper over to Red Paper and make the Green worthless after a certain date, Gold and Silver would get you far more of the new Red Paper than large quantities of the Green.

People have been conditioned to think of Gold and Silver as just another Stock or Commodity to try their hand at investing in. They watch to see whether it will go up or down in value. Those who invested in Gold in the early 2,000's at around $300 per ounce were thrilled to see its Price move to over $1,800 per ounce. Those, however, that didn't purchase until it was almost $1,800 felt like losers when it fell back to around $1,200.

What most fail to consider is that Gold has not changed at all. An ounce of Gold then is an ounce of Gold now. It didn't grow or appreciate in value it is a value itself. The Money is what lost value, as if it had any to begin with, inflating it causes Prices to rise. Lost confidence in it also causes people to require more of it to persuade them to use it at all. One ounce of Gold in the early 2000's bought 300 Federal Reserve Notes and later that same one ounce could buy 1,800 Federal Reserve Notes so one could conclude that Federal Reserve Notes really went down in Price during that time period. Maybe one should pay more attention to whether a particular Currency is a good or bad investment rather than the other way around.

While ignorance continues to hold Paper in its place as "Money" the wise should at least hold Gold and Silver as a "Hedge" rather than an investment against the inherent risk in such a system. A "Hedge" is a means of protection against financial lose. Using Gold and Silver as a counterbalance against the risk of lost purchasing power and other political disaster prone to affect Fiat Paper Money could save you from financial ruin.

By holding 25 to 30% percent of your liquid wealth in Gold and Silver you could be insured against economic disaster and upheavals. While your so-called "Gold Investment" is not increasing or even diminishing some, as measured in Paper Dollars, you know the confidence in Paper remains and the other economic activities you are involved in are going fine. You are employed, eating well and although Gold will not get you extra Paper Dollars you are content that an ounce of Gold remains an ounce and doesn't shrink. Should the economy go bad, unemployment rise and other investments become shaky the Gold "Hedge" will pay off big time by suddenly having the purchasing power and then some of all your other holding that have gone bad.

As a real-life example take a person that followed the above suggestion in the early 2000's by taking $100,000 and using 25% percent to buy Gold as a "Hedge" against his investment and use of the other $75,000. The $25,000 (25% hedge) would have bought 83 one-ounce Gold coins at that time. Since that time to this day interest rates have been almost non-existent but let us assume the $75,000 was invested and a rate of 7% percent interest was achieved. After eight years this investment would have reached a total of $128,864. At this point the Real Estate and Banking crisis was in full swing. Although this particular crisis probably did not cause our investor to lose the entire $128,864, he had accrued, but even if it had his "Hedge" with Gold would have completely covered the loss. The 83 one-ounce coins having reached a Price of over $1,800 per coin for a total of over $150,000.

If this investor chose not to "Hedge" with gold holdings and rather investing the whole $100,000 at the assumed rate this would have amounted to $171,816. If the crises had only set his value back as little as 13% percent, he would have fared better investing the lesser amount and holding the Hedge. Had he been fully invested in Gold (real Money) at the time of the crisis his investment would have been worth over $600,000.

In the earlier days of our Country a person could take the Gold he mined in the hills to the U.S. Treasury and have it mint for a small fee into coins or he could deposit it and receive a Certificate of Deposit a receipt which looks much like today's Dollar Bills only it could be redeemed at any time for the actual Gold or Silver on deposit. At that time Congress had set the value of a Dollar to a specific number of grains of Gold a number that made a one ounce Gold piece worth $20.

Since disconnecting from the Dollar as a specific measure that once made an ounce of Gold and a $20 Dollar Bill an equivalent value, we are now faced with Dollar Bills (in name only) 1,800 of which have recently been required to have the same value as that one-ounce Gold coin.

It would be outlandish if you went to the store for a gallon of milk one week and upon returning to buy another gallon the following week found it to be half the size of last week. Or having bought a pound of meat this week to find they are claiming a pound is half the number of ounces it was last week. What if as a farmer you sold corn to the grocer for $2 per bushel and when you came to do so again found the containers much larger but still called a bushel and paying the same $2. Wouldn't you be outraged? How would you plan? How would you know if you were gaining or losing if gallons and pounds varied in the number of their ounces? What if yards varied in the number of feet considered a yard from one month to the next? If you went to buy a yard of three feet of fabric and received only two feet?

The above paints a ridiculous picture. How would things function without standards? Without weights and measures being set standards, with all required to abide by them and be responsible for the claims they make, there would be chaos. So why is there no cry for a set standard of Value? Why can a Dollar be one thing this week and another the next and no one be upset about it? Until Congress does its job, as with other units of measure, economic chaos will impoverish many and unduly enrich others allowed to manipulate the value of our Money and Labor and influence the Price of our Goods.

With a set value for our Money and a reliable measure of wealth Money itself would cease to be more desirable than real wealth itself, the goods and services that Money can buy. Having Money of a set reliable value would ensure that savings would buy the same amount of goods tomorrow as they can today. It would make goods just as valuable in the hands of the consumer as it was when it was in the hands of the producer. It would reward productivity but not require a frantic pace that if not kept would cause collapse.

To show why these things are true we need to contrast the two systems. Currently if Supply and Demand for a particular item are at equilibrium and have arrived at a given Price if the Money Supply is increased then Price will also increase or if the Money Supply is decreased then Price will also decrease.

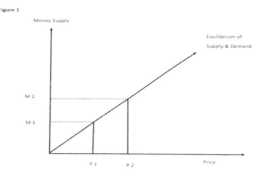

Figure 1

Under the same current system if Money Supply and Price are at equilibrium then if Production Supply increases then Price decreases if Production Supply decreases then Price increases. Under this same equilibrium if Demand increases then Price also increases if Demand decreases then Price decreases.

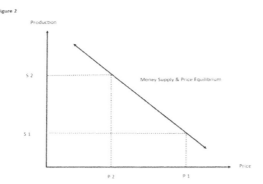

Figure 2

The problem here beside the unjust enrichment of the Money Men is that these variations in direction of Price are counter to proper incentive to production and the welfare of the people. You will note as shown in Fig. 2 above that as more Production is Supplied the Price falls. Therefore, for unemployment to be solved and to seek for all who wish to be productive to have a place under the current system it would occur at the cost of making everyone's labor less rewarding. By Prices dropping the profit or increase available to those who participate is diminished, reducing incentive. Conversely when participation is dropping off, less people working and producing, a reduction in Product Supply causes Prices to rise; this when the people can least afford it.

As we have seen, and Fig. 2 shows, when Demand for a Product rises so does its Price. This rise in Price has the effect of discouraging the Demand that has begun. This may be a desirable occurrence for a natural resource or a material in short supply that needs to be conserved but

102

for an industry with no supply problem desiring to grow and whose owners, managers and workers wish to share in increased wealth, discouraging Demand is not the goal. But as we have also seen above adding workers and increasing Production Supply produces a disincentive with falling Prices and devalued labor.

What's needed is a reversal in incentive where increased Production Supply and increased Demand for the Supply is not met with ever increasing Price and reductions in the incentive to produce by devaluing labor.

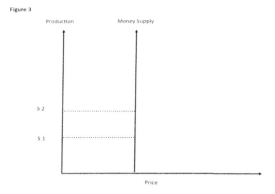

Figure 3

With a Monetary System not based on Debt increased Production Supply is an increase in wealth. As more goods are created more is available to all without anyone being indebted for the privilege of being allowed to produce. With a corresponding increase in the Supply of Money to represent the increased wealth (the Production Supply) Price would remain stable as shown in Fig. 3.

The usual reactions of Prices rising with increasing Money Supply is counterbalanced by the usual reaction of increased Production Supply causing Prices to fall. By stabilizing Prices, you allow for increased Production without a loss of value in the goods or labor of the people so wealth can increase for all. Productivity is rewarded rather than punished and with the value of goods and property maintained, Money is not more desirable than real wealth (the goods and things that people use). This makes goods as valuable in the hands of the consumer as in the hands of the producer. It also allows for full employment for all who desire it without destruction of Prices and without diminishing the value of all other laborers. This in turn means that you do not increase poverty in the midst of plenty as with our current system.

Since the value of labor and the value of goods are maintained along with stable Prices there is no disincentive to Savings. If what you save aside today doesn't lose its purchasing power or value then being frugal can be a benefit. Additionally planned obsolescence does not need to be built into products so good quality lasting products can again be produced. The economy does not need to have ever increasing rates of production in order to prevent implosion. Ever increasing need does not have to be perpetuated requiring continuous loans and credit extension in order to maintain a Supply of the Medium of Exchange in circulation. The circulation of Honest Money remains in circulation for continuous transactions; it is not vacuumed out by the endless need to pay off Debt and Usury Interest.

Honest Money eliminates the booms and busts of Inflation and Deflation. Although some Price changes are inevitable the cause of these changes in one commodity, or another would not be due to the manipulation of Money and Credit by corrupt men. They would be isolated occurrences and not across the board trends. They would occur due to actual changes in the circumstances of Supply and Demand of a particular commodity. As previously described such events as destroyed crops, sparse yields or unusually abundant seasons can have their effect on Prices and are a Free Markets natural response to equalize Supply with the Demand.

Occurrences of rapid Appreciation or Depreciation would be rare. The increase of wealth occurring largely by being productive and supplying quality goods and services to others and not by being unduly enriched at the expense of others and their losses. The only drawbacks to a Debt free Honest Money System are for those Money Men currently enriching themselves on the misery of the people, their cronies and the shiftless person who wants something for nothing. If you are not among that group, you will extol the changes.

CHAPTER 9

Debt Free Money

People's idea of Money today is so entangled with the concepts of Inflation, Deflation, Credit and Interest that I think the advantages and changes that Honest Money would precipitate are difficult to imagine. After years of being on the treadmill and juggling payments the words in the last chapter alone probably do not leave you with a clear picture of what such change would mean for all.

The idea that the Medium of Exchange used by all to facilitate the exchange of goods and services with each other would not be owed back to anybody is revolutionary. You would be hard pressed to find in our Country or any other a person alive today who has not lived since birth under a Debt Based Money System.

Imagine Our Country with zero National Debt and a population of Citizens most of whom could not say they even know a person who is in Debt. A Country where everyone who wanted to work and produce or serve could. Where small and large businesses consisted mainly of owners with profit sharing employee partners because doing otherwise made it too difficult to obtain skilled and steady workers, who otherwise had other options. All this industry occurring at a steady but leisurely pace because taking a break wouldn't cause you to be out run by Debt collectors and Interest Rates. Where paychecks were not divided up by the number of monthly payments. Where competition in industry would not be won by the biggest liar or fastest producer of junk but rather the best service provider and the maker of long-lasting quality products.

Am I describing a dream or a fantasy? Only if we continue further into Debt and toward Doomsday. But if we make the change to Honest Money described in the previous chapter the above is not only possible but the natural outcome and result that many didn't catch while reading the previous chapter. The consequences of the Debt Based Corruption we have been living under is so insidious that we have come to see the chains we live with as normal and the natural result of honesty and integrity and doing rightly to our neighbor as a far-fetched fantasy.

With an intrinsically valued Medium of Exchange that is not Debt Based when you are paid you are not receiving an IOU but actual wealth. You may spend it again in exchange for real wealth in a different form such as food, clothing or tools or you may save it aside until such a time that those items are desired.

You may be thinking that you can do that with to-day's IOU's also. But today's IOU's cannot be saved safely. When you save them aside you risk there not being as valuable later as when you received them. It is not a matter of if they will change value but only when and how fast. Being that they enter circulation by being loaned in. That type of Money Supply is always either expanding or contracting it cannot be otherwise.

Honest Money is paid to you by another who owns it in exchange for something different that someone else owns; and on and on it goes remaining a part of the vast wealth held by all the people as a whole. Since it is not sucked out of circulation to pay it back to Bankers along with added Interest there is no shortage of its availability to participate in yet more and more transactions.

Because there is not a shortage of the Medium of Exchange to be used in transactions that means if you have a willingness to labor and produce a good or service and someone else has a desire to have that good or service the transaction can occur.

Think about how radical a concept that really is against that which occurs today. Today no matter how willing to work and produce a person may be it sometimes take weeks or even months after losing one job to find another. Even if they know many people and have lots of friends and relatives often no one is able to offer them work. Their own budgets and fixed incomes prevent them. Leaving them just feeling lucky they are not in the same position. Maybe this person is a carpenter and a friend of his would really love a new porch or other home addition, despite having desire and willingness on both sides of the transaction it is prevented by lack of the available Medium of Exchange.

The only thing preventing a remedy to the above situation and millions of others like it is the lack of sufficient supply of Money in Circulation. So, if as we have shown that real wealth is the goods and services that Money can purchase and if we have no shortage of the goods, services and labor to produce wealth why is the proper amount of Money not supplied to us to allow this wealth to be exchanged with each other? There is only the reason that some worship Money, Power and Control and these corrupt men have conspired by force, manipulation, fraud and bribery to entrench themselves and their minions into positions of Power to further their Control and accumulation of riches.

Would Honest Debt Free Money mean the end of Banking, Lending and Credit? Not at all! It would mean the end of Lending the Money Supply into circulation to provide it as a Medium of Exchange. It would mean the end of Usury Interest Rates and the end of Fractional Reserve Banking. Money and Credit would not be allowed to be extended out of thin air as this is not Lending but stealing as has been shown. Banks would return to being a place to safely hold savings and to protect stores of silver, gold and other valuables. They could still be the facilitators of Money Transfers between individuals and industry, accounting for the Debits and Credits of account holders with others. Simple fee-based lending could be facilitated by them but only from the savings and accumulations of others willing to lend it and take the risks. Risks not shared by the People as a whole but by the risk takers themselves.

Applications for a loan by someone seeking Credit would be approved or disapproved by the willing lenders themselves unless they wished to delegate such authority to a Banker or other agent. Good Credit Ratings would be based on a person's integrity and record of repayment not on the amount of Usury Interest previously extracted from them. If loans went bad Banks would be no more or less stable as only the accounts of the individual lenders, risk takers, would be Debited.

Credit Cards would be largely just Debit Cards against Bank saving and checking accounts. For actual Credit Cards investor pools of real Money would be collected from actual savers who wished to share in such risk for certain fees, although maximum rates would apply to prevent Usury.

Business loans would occur on the same basis of identifiable lenders willing to risk their own Capital (Savings). Capitalization for Corporations would come from Stockholder Investment and risk of loss against shared profits. No business would be too big to fail. Improper management and failure would be born only by those involved, the gap in the Market to be filled by competitors or other risk takers. The Stock Market would cease to be a den of gamblers wagering other people's Money and return to being a location for the pooling of Capital for industry and a place for the Marketing of goods.

With a sufficient Supply of Money in circulation the need to borrow or extend Credit would be almost nonexistent for most individuals paying and receiving payment for their production and labor as they go. Credit and lending procedures described above would be largely for the expansion of industry and business and for the purpose of bringing opportunity and wealth to ever increasing numbers. The failure to obtain Credit or convince others of a viable business venture would not affect an individual's ability to provide the necessities of life to themselves and their families.

In fact, presupposing that a demand by the People to move to Honest Money would also mean a move to Honest Government it could be pointed out that the elimination of taxes on property and a prohibition on its confiscation would virtually cease the increase of poverty in the Nation. Anyone having accumulated wealth enough to meet their own level of satisfaction could take their leisure or retirement without fear of its depletion by the need to meet confiscatory taxes of by an ever-shrinking Monetary Value.

To make plain how a sufficient Supply of Honest Money increases the wealth of all let us look at a small microcosm of society much the same way we did in order to show Usury Lending by the Banker to our three early settlers in a previous chapter was in fact stealing. Remember that we also previously showed that adding to the Supply of Money faster than the creation of new goods caused Inflation a symptom of which is rising Prices. This because more Money starts chasing fewer goods. What I am here proposing is that adding Money so long as you are also adding more goods causes Prices to remain the same. This because Inflationary effect of more Money is offset by the usual Deflationary effect of increased Production Supply. So therefore, more Money at the same time as more goods allows more for all without the drawback of reducing the value of goods and labor of those already involved leaving an incentive rather that a disincentive to increase wealth.

If we take an extremely small economy with just four participants just as we did when showing in the earlier example that the Money Supplier, the Banker, was stealing from the others you will see the difference with Money of Intrinsic Value. So, we have in this case our Gold Miner who comes to the Market with four gold coins he has labored to produce. Next comes our Farmer with four bushels of corn, our Tailor with four sets of clothes and lastly our Rancher with four slabs of meat all having labored to produce their goods.

Figure #1

Our Farmer could exchange directly (Barter) with any of the others and vice versa without the need of the Miner's coins to do so because of the size and proximity of this Marketplace. For the sake of applying this example to a greater economy where I have already shown a Medium of Exchange (Money) to be necessary let us begin with the coined Money being exchanged and use it exclusively in each exchange.

Therefore, we begin by having our Gold Miner use his coins to purchase his needs from each of the other Market participants. So, our Miner pays one coin to each of the others in exchange for some of each item changing the holdings of each as shown in Figure # 2 below where each is seen to now have one coin and three items of which they brought remaining. Except the Miner who has one coin remaining and one of each of the other items.

Figure #2

Next the Farmer and the Tailor each spend their coin with the Rancher for his meat with the result shown below in Figure # 3 with the Rancher having one slab of meat remaining and three coins while the Farmer and Tailor each have meat and three of their own products remaining.

Figure #3

Now our Rancher spends two of his coins to get the other items he needs so like the Minor now has one of each item for his needs. The Farmer and Tailor each having a coin, meat and two of their own products as shown in Figure # 4 below.

Figure #4

So now in the final transaction the Farmer and Tailor each purchase an item from each other leaving all Market participants with one item of their own and one each from the other Market participants as shown below in Figure # 5.

Figure #5

Our microcosm of society in the earlier chapter exposed the Bankers larceny and gave a view of it that is very difficult to see when looking at the greater picture of millions of daily transactions. You should note in this microcosm of society that the needs of each were met with no one left in Debt at the end of transactions. Everyone's needs were met. Further a sufficient number of coins provided for that to occur in fewer transactions than would have been the case if less coins were available although with Honest Money the end result would be the same.

If we now imagine that each of our participants go back to producing more goods prior to another visit to the Marketplace, then at their next visit the same can be done all over again. At each visit to the Market place our producers are all not only varying the makeup of their wealth but increasing it as well. When you now enlarge the society to millions of participants in millions of transactions over thousands of the various goods and services available to meet the needs and wants of the participants you have a true Free Market.

CHAPTER 10

Proper Government

Along with the need for an Honest Money Supply a happy and prosperous people need a Righteous and Honest Government. Just as people suffer at the hands of dishonest men in control of the Medium of Exchange they suffer when these same or similar men hold seats of administration within Government. Seldom, if ever, does the breakdown of Government begin with the people. Disrespect for the Law and opposition to those who administer it is usually the result of people becoming aware of corruption and inefficiency in high places. People under tyrannical Governments suffer oppression and are subject to unjust laws and administration regardless of the Natural Resources and wealth of a Nation. People living under lawful Government have administrators who administer the Law for the benefit of all so that righteousness and justice may be established, refusing to favor any one group or class over another.

The forefathers of America expressed the real purpose of Government when they wrote the preamble of the Constitution. "We the people of the united States, in order to form a more perfect union, establish justice, insure domestic tranquility, provide for the common defense, promote the general welfare, and secure the blessings of liberty to ourselves and our posterity, do ordain and establish this constitution of the United States of America."

It is impossible to have domestic tranquility unless there be equitable taxation, which is not confiscation of property, and unless there is a proper distribution of the right to labor and possess wealth. Laws must be administered that are just to all, from the humblest to the greatest of all Citizens. Governments in business and business controlling Government destroy the very purpose of Government itself.

The one and only purpose of government is to prevent violence and crime and to enforce the keeping of law and order. Even national defense is in essence the prevention of violence and crime. When governments depart from protecting the Citizens and their property and liberty and assume rights and functions never intended to be exercised by governing bodies the result has always been tyranny and oppression as is evidenced by history and in current government activities shown by the evils of our numerous bureaucracies.

If you were to poll people on the streets today and ask them "What form of Government do we have here in America?" the majority of those, who even had an answer, would declare "a Democracy". Is a "Democracy" what the founding fathers established? Have you ever said the pledge of allegiance to the Flag? If so, you will note it is to the Flag and to the Republic for which it stands that we pledge allegiance! We were given a

Republic by those that established this Country. Although we have democratic procedures a Democracy as a form of government was abhorred by most of the founders as being mob rule. Democracy is a form of government that is suicidal and always ends badly. A government by the people which the final court of appeal is public opinion. Socialism is that phase of democracy which negates property rights and anarchy the phase which negates law.

A Republic on the other hand is a government with Representatives of the People carrying out the administration of Law. Law outlined in a constitution adhering to authority and principles held above even the majority. In the case of America those rights unalienable and endowed to us by the Almighty Creator. Among them the right to life, liberty and property. Others outlined in the first ten amendments as the Bill of Rights that certain States demanded be included lest they refuse ratification.

Not only did the founders believe in these Rights given us by the Almighty but they proclaimed them to be self-evident. This means they do not even need arguing that everyone should see them as plain as the light of day. In fact, every elected official and public position holder takes an oath to uphold the Constitution. That means everyone that violates these principles or works against them while in office perjures their oath and commits a felony.

As was pointed out in a previous chapter Rights cannot be taxed without converting them from Rights to Privileges. If these Rights are unalienable and endowed, given, to us by the Almighty then no man no matter what position he holds has a right to take them from us. No matter what he decrees or writes even if he calls that decree or writing Law it is not. He may declare a thing or action legal and may direct men with guns to enforce it and although he may possess the power to coerce and enforce he remains without lawful authority. Tyranny, as a rule, arises from within a nation when the Government has been captured by men who would use their acquired power to oppress the People. Therefore the *Right* to keep and bear arms was among those articulated in the Constitution. Every man in a free nation should be counted among its defenders and hold and keep the instrument of his arms and equipment in his own possession.

Now the Right of Citizens to keep and bear arms is fundamental in preserving true freedom, so much so that subversive forces in sundry and subtle ways first move to disarm the Citizens of a nation which they later plan to dominate. We already have unconstitutional laws violating Article II in many States all done under the pretext of disarming the criminal. The criminal, who never disarms, knows he is dealing with law-abiding unarmed citizens. Honest men and leaders never fear an armed, law-abiding, civilian population. Evil men, however, will always fear the righteous indignation of a people able to defend their homes, their freedom and their liberty whenever it is threatened.

All wealth comes from the land. Everything your eye beholds at one time, or another came from dirt, rocks, water and trees. Without property and the rights to it men cannot be free or produce wealth and maintain life. That is why men have instituted governments in the first place to protect them and their families from those who would enslave them or take their life. That is why government cannot be the Protector of Property Rights and the taker of Property at the same time. Either Property Rights are held inviolable, or they are not. To tax or punish a man by confiscation of property is to punish and steal from not only him but his family and its generations.

To tax property as previously explained is to slowly whittle away or eventually steal all that he has. Therefore, Honest and Proper Government has no Property Tax and consequently no Inheritance Tax. A man's land and home once owned should be free from tax and confiscation for any reason. This protection should extend to include the last of food, clothing and bedding. Making restitution for his misdeeds and debts may apply to all else beyond these as well as the rights to the fruit of his labor and include the production from his land and property until such time restitution is complete, forgiven or until the maximum time of set release. These criteria, firm and set, as the expectations of all would govern lenders and others in their transactions with one another knowing the extent to which recovery was possible.

Then how is Government to be funded? By recognizing the limited role of government, it will be apparent that the vast amounts of Money expended by it today would not be needed. A government that provides law and order and protection of the Citizens and their Property and sets standards of weights, measures and value of the Medium of Exchange yet refrains from the endless creation of bureaucracies on every other topic and aspect of our lives will be lean and mean. It is not governments place to educate our children, see to our retirements, govern our health care, choose what our farmers grow, subsidize Corporations, fund research or to even provide charity.

For instance, America is and always has been the most giving nation on earth. It raises and gives billions to relief efforts for disasters and the poor around the world. In a world led by the example of an Honest Money Supply the poor in America would be few. Far fewer than today where welfare and food stamp numbers continue to grow despite the vast sums spent by Government on fighting it. Private organizations and the major religions all have much less costly and more efficient systems for providing for the needs of the poor than government. Might they require the recipient to hear their message or make an assessment about steps that could be taken to change their situation? Yes! Is there something wrong with having expectations regarding a person's own willingness to help themselves when you are about to provide for them, that which they have been unable to provide for themselves? I think not and the evidence shows the Governments unconditional program has led to nothing but increased need and dependence. When Church's and other private organizations give charity, it is actually charity provided by individuals who give freely. When governments give so-called charity, it is actually stolen or misappropriated funds. Taxes which are mandatory and extracted from some and given to others is not charity. Forced giving last I checked was considered robbery.

Suffice it to say that endless examples of the evils and injustice of government going outside its main function and how it enriches some while impoverishing many are endless. Endless also are the evils that can be cited by the Big Government Advocate about men of business and their manipulation, price fixing and monopolizing of Capital Markets. I agree wholly but I would contend that Honest Money and Proper Government would tend toward smaller and greater choices in Companies servicing the economy. It is the undue enrichment of some caused by government that places them in a position to monopolize industry in the first place. Additionally, if governments function of unbiased enforcing of the Law and punishing the corrupt came quickly and surely other men would fear to duplicate such acts. It is wholly due to special influence and entangled government interests that injustice and delayed justice occurs in the quantities that we have seen.

But let's return to my main aim in a discussion on Government. Proper Government and the arguments for and against its participation in certain areas could require a book of its own. My main point here is to show that the evils of a corrupt Money System cannot be overcome by a change to Honest Money alone; for the very reason it was corruption and ignorance in government that led to the allowance of Fiat Money in the first place. Whether or not it is Bankers or Government or both that confiscate the wealth of the People matters not as misery is still occurring. Honest Money of a set value will prevent the Bankers, but only certain sound principles of administration will restrain the Government.

The first and foremost of these principles beyond that of Honest Money itself is inviolable respect for property ownership. The second is just taxation. Taxation must be fair and applicable to all. It has been shown already that taxing property is to confiscate it whether slowly or speedily the only difference. It should also be recognized that all taxes are paid by the people individually and that fictitious entities such as Corporations, LLC's, Trusts and a host of other organizational types do no pay taxes because they are not living breathing beings. The taxing of these creations of man and government only serve to confuse the issue of who is paying the tax and how much is being paid. Only the individuals who own or manage these organizations or those that they pass it off on end up paying the taxes purported to be on the organization itself.

Let's face it a corporation that makes and sells a product for $2 and is then taxed by government, after some politician has promised to make the Corporation pay their fair share, does nothing more than add the additional tax to the Price of its product. The people now pay $3 for the product not realizing that the politician increased their taxes because he didn't do it directly. Now this is not to say that appropriate fees to cover the costs associated with the Governments cost of administration in the registration of Corporations should not be charged and born by those utilizing such tools of business themselves. But let us not delude ourselves in the other greater principles. Those who create the costs should pay them. The cost of Government protecting the people and their property should be borne by all who benefit as well.

A tax on *Increase* is a tax that can be fairly paid by all. If I provide protection for you and your property so that you are free to put all your effort into increasing the wealth of you and your family then I would think it only fair to receive payment to cover my cost of doing so and thereby allow me to benefit my own family. So, if collectively we do this very thing for each other by the institution of government then it is only right to share in that cost.

The rich have more to protect and the poor less. If you think you are without the need of such protection you are out of touch with the realities of life and its thieves, aggressive men and murderers who refrain from such activities only by their assessment of the odds of being punished. Therefore, by each paying a portion of that increase they have been enabled to produce, the costs of government can be funded. This is done with the additional benefit that the Government's interests become aligned with that of the People's. For the more the Citizen increases the more the Government's revenue. If government is made to spend only within its means just as any family or individual must, then incentives line up together with more for the People meaning more for the Government. This being a third principal government living within its means, a Balanced Budget!

Now I can already hear the arguments of the various tax proponents and opponents of each of today's taxing schemes from VAT Taxes to Sales Taxes to the Graduated Income Tax all have their arguments for and against each. All these taxes have serious flaws in implementation and enforcement as well as various groups and individuals unable to escape as others easily escape responsibility.

I am aware that the Income Tax in this Country has never been properly ratified or lawfully applied and through legal terms of art, trick many more Citizens to whom it ever applied into voluntary compliance and self-assessment. But this does not change the fact that an Income Tax fairly applied would be the least resisted by the population.

Done right it would be the least costly and the least intrusive to administer and patriotism and a sense of honesty would make it the most voluntarily complied with tax in history. I am not talking about the grossly unfair progressive and socialist Income Tax System we currently bear up under. A progressive Income Tax is a "steal from the rich give to the government and the poor" system. But an across-the-board tax on increase, measured by value and applied equally to Rich and Poor alike with no loopholes and no deductions would be simple and fair. If for example all paid a tax of 10 percent of their

Income, then a person making a million would pay $100,000 and a person making $100,000 would pay $10,000 and a poorer person making $10,000 would pay $1,000. This way the Rich would indeed pay more than the Poor in dollars but the same in percentage. No deductions for the various uses Income were put to would apply as all would be free to use their after tax remainder anyway they saw fit, it being now their inviolably protected property.

The increased compliance due to fairness and simplicity alone would benefit the costs of administration and change any current Pride of beating the system to an unpatriotic shame instead. Businesses of course would continue to deduct the costs involved with producing their (Income) profits. Being that it is understood that taxing them separately is just a hidden tax on the people, certain set amounts of Retained Earnings would be established to allow for Company growth plans along with an amount based on a percentage of Capital Assets and their need for replacement. Income above these amounts would either be distributed as dividends to the individual owners or if held and credited to the Capital Accounts of said owners, with the tax born by the individual account holder who would pay currently just as a Limited Partner does today.

Additional revenue and cost coverage would come from Imposts and Duties set at our borders and ports for the foreigner to share the cost of security and administration and for the privilege of access to our Marketplace. This would serve as a governor to pressure or reward foreign governments for their economic policies. For example, a country seeking to undermine a market here with the introduction of inferior goods or those produced at reduced cost due to slave labor would see fees causing them the necessity of raising their Prices to meet or exceed those they had planned to undermine here. This would eliminate the advantage of using such labor. Countries that allowed our products to freely compete in their Markets would be reciprocated by us in our Market.

Is this protectionism? Certainly, it is but since when is protecting our families and our Country a bad thing? Is it not the very function for which government was instituted in the first place? Governments very function is to protect its Citizen's interests, punish criminals, protect property and set the system of true weights, measures, volumes and values to be adhered to by all. A Government that remains focused and bound by its legitimate functions is one that is unbiased, just, lean and efficient.

For those who do not believe that the revenues outlined thus far would support the Government sufficiently have probably been living under the struggle caused by Fiat Money so long they cannot fathom the amount of wealth and prosperity such a system would bring about. But for the nay Sayers I have saved an Income Source that will out due all the others mentioned thus far. Of course, the outcry, opposition and rhetoric of those currently grossly over enriched, at the loss of the People, will be as loud as that of the Central Bankers to the abolition of Paper Money. To whom do I refer? Well in many cases they may be some of the same men as those in our Central Banks, but I refer to their cronies within Private Corporations. As the means to steal all our individual wealth was given to the Bankers with the Money Press the same means was given to Private hands to take the wealth belonging to the Nation and the People as a whole. What wealth is that? It is the wealth of our Natural Resources.

Why are private individuals and companies owning and controlling the Natural Resources of our Country? If our Country is "We the People" why is someone else enjoying our wealth? No, I am not proposing Socialism nor Communism in any way. Nowhere in this book have I advocated for anything other than private property and individual Rights. But just as Corporations hold assets owned by their multiple Stockholders the Natural Resources of a Nation are Corporately held assets of the Citizens of the Nation and not the private holdings of a few privileged men.

The water, the rain, sea and rivers, oil, gas, the minerals of the mountains and hills and the natural production of field and forest apart from man's labor represent the wealth of a nation and its people. Why are individuals and small groups taking possession of this wealth and allowed to make billions and billions of dollars for themselves from the property of all? Recently while Citizens were struggling with the highest gas prices in history Private Corporations were reporting quarterly profits of billions of dollars. Mind you that these profits by the very definition of profit meant this was income over and above the costs of the Company. Costs that include finding it, extracting it, paying all the workers who labored for it and multi-million-dollar executive salaries and benefit packages all deductible expenses prior to the declaration of the profits. These profits could be used to either lessen the cost of the People's purchases of the product itself or be delivered to the government treasury to offset the cost of government or both.

I am fully aware of the issues of inefficiencies, waste, shortage, lack of quality and incentive in not only Socialist and Communist governments, who control resources through public or government utilities, but even in our own. As stated previously government does not belong in business.

Private enterprise and industry should receive adequate compensation and profit-sharing incentives for the conversion of our Natural Resources into usable production, but the National Treasury should receive adequate returns from these assets that all the People may share in our national wealth. This should not be done in the form of a Corporate Tax whereas shown the Corporation just adds its costs to the Price paid by the people. It should instead be a formula of percentages where costs are covered and all proceeds beyond that split between labor, management, government and the People. This way putting all participants on the same incentive program of reduced costs, quality, efficiency and conservation. In this way travesties such as ruined health, ruined landscape and poverty as in West Virginia with the coal miners and their land would never occur. The extra profits to management could not occur without the proportional benefits to the other participants as well.

Under this system the Government would be more than adequately funded and with aligned interests of government, the People and industry regulation, conservation, replenishment and environmental issues would be balanced. Mismanagement or over-regulation would affect all parties equally. Over-regulation costs would reduce government intake as much as industries and mismanagement or lack of environmental concern would be as costly to industry as to those complaining about it. This would bring balance as well as incentive for industry to further profit by creating jobs and managing the environmental, conservation and replenishing industry as well.

It's hard to imagine for some, how we would cope without government micromanaging and regulating every aspect of our lives. Many would point to the horrible factory conditions and abuse of workers, child labor, unlicensed Doctors etc.. etc.. and on and on. But they would also ignore that these abuses came from the very issues of controlled and manipulated Money and its supply, from government corruption bending to special interests and the fact that government intervention in areas not their function always causes injustice, impoverishment of many and the enrichment of a few.

However, if government stuck to the business of law and order and protection of property bringing swift and certain justice to violators would diminish criminal activity rapidly. If Money was Honest the necessities of life would be abundant, and no man would have to sacrifice himself to poor factory conditions or inferior pay for his time to see to the survival of his family.

Such things as license and quality assurance and building codes could all be for profit private industry provided without the need of government to restrict the rights of all to prevent the abuse of a few. If the penalty for stealing, fraud and other damages to your neighbor included restitution in full, crime would also diminish quickly. What good is putting a lazy thief in jail to cost society even more than was stolen in the first place all the while feeding, clothing and providing TV. Other than a possible vindictive pleasure in the fact the thief was caught, nothing of the lost was returned to the victim. If, however, the thief had to face who he stole from and replace double the value taken or work the time neces- sary to do so, it would save society as a whole, cost the thief and reimburse the victim.

On the topic of consumer protection or quality it was once upon a time when the saying "Caveat Emptor" meaning "Buyer Beware" was the order of the day. Meaning some critical thinking and assessment is our own responsibility but where this is not enough, and real damage occurs swift justice and actual restitution would go far to rectify it. Additionally, the private industry of Certifications, Consumer Reports and Complaint Bureaus could do wonders as well as creating jobs and leaving freedom intact. Such Companies as Underwriters Laboratories exist for manufacturers willing to stand behind their products. They can send products to be tested and rated proudly displaying the UL approved decal that the consumer trusts. If such Companies succumb to bribery or payment for ratings type policies consumers will lose confidence in their ratings and seek products certified by companies known for their integrity.

Driver's licenses could be accomplished in similar manner. Many may feel otherwise but for the sake of creative thinking and to see restriction of rights is not always the answer let's assume it was not a government function. Remember we are under a government of law and order that protects citizen's property rights. That means if you take your car down the road and cause an accident you will be liable for the damage you cause to the person and property of others.

Remember also that being a lazy person of no wealth at all will not get you a pass simply because you can't afford the damages you cause. Well knowing these things, you would be wise to actually have practiced and know how to drive. If you worry you could still cause damage by making a mistake you couldn't afford. Then you might purchase some insurance to be safe. When you go to buy it, they might ask if you have taken a driver's education course from one of several Certified Companies. When you tell them no, they quote you an insurance premium you can hardly afford. After complaint they inform you if you take a course at one of the Certified Companies, they will lower the cost of insurance by 75% percent. So, you decide this is best and do so and obtain good driving skills and low insurance costs to protect against the off chance of an accident.

Although free to do otherwise prudence caused you to become a Certified and insured driver. A bank loaning Money to buy a car might require insurance to protect its investment and although free to be unlicensed the same insurance issue caused you to get certified anyway. All this without making it a law that you get a license. With such a law that government would need another bureaucracy, agents and a budget. Crazy you think? People wouldn't do it there would just be more accidents you think? Remember our limited government is well funded for that which it does do and that is protect people's property interests. So, when your friend Joe tells you he didn't bother with insurance or learning to drive properly and after his accident he now owes thousands as a judgment and is being forced to work a job he hates until it's all paid off you may change your mind.

You may think this discussion on proper government has taken a turn far afield of Honest Money, but it is important to show that without a limited government of sound principles even Honest Money will be difficult to retain and happiness difficult to come by. It is my hope to get the creative juices flowing and see that government was never meant to be our savior and provider of all answers. Although it's important that wrong doers are punished swiftly and victims compensated surely it is not governments place to make us right thinkers, politically correct speakers or even unprejudiced individuals. We are free to think anything we want and have whatever attitude we choose. Certain attitudes may bring us fewer or greater interactions with others, but we are not to act out certain bad behavior.

Murder, rape, kidnapping, larceny, assault and battery are all unlawful actions no matter what the reason for them. If I hit you over the head to steal your wallet because you are fat, gay or a different color it doesn't matter the reason, one is not better than another, the action (behavior) is unlawful and to be punished. If I don't like people of another color or if they are fat no amount of government regulation is going to make me nor is any needed because if I act out in any unlawful way the laws to punish such behavior already exist and more names for them and additional agencies to enforce them is a waste.

The last subject I'll touch on before returning directly to that of Honest Money in circulation is War. Every instance of War is costly and can never be measured in dollars alone because of the many irreplaceable lives that are lost in them. Without going into any depth or proofs I would submit that to have the People, industry and government all lined up with shared interests as is the case with proper government principles that I have outlined the decision to War would not be taken lightly, would affect all equally and prevent that decision being made by special interests and Money men. Those principles being Honest Money, Inviolable respect for Property Rights, Just Taxation and a Government that lives within its means on a Balances Budget.

CHAPTER 11

Measure of Value

It is my hope at this point that you have a much clearer picture of the reasons for the financial chaos and the economic hardships experienced by so many today. That you recognize the schemes of the Money Lenders and how they serve themselves on the misery of others. How they use the riches they accumulated to derail the sound principles of proper government to further increase their power and wealth. It has not been my aim in this writing to name the names of the perpetrators or the specific where, when and how's of the infiltration but rather to make you aware of the principle tenants of their fraud itself.

It is impossible to fix an engine if you do not know how it runs. The schemers will continue their scam so long as People fail to understand there even is a scam. To think our economy is just a hodge-podge of haphazard actions by good intentioned politicians who can never seem to agree on the next step is to miss the systematic fleecing and direction of those seeking world domination. If you are interested in the who's who of culprits, the time and dates of their principal events and the methods employed there are many good books that do just that which I have listed a few of in the Appendixes at the back of this book.

Recognizing the scam and how it works will go further to reversing the problem than memorizing the names and players who initially started the ball rolling. Additionally having some idea about what is proper, and right is absolutely necessary to changing the current mess into a just and equitable system. Changing from bad to worse is not an option at this late and critical point in their plan.

An honest system is so diametrically opposed to the current corruption stopping on the dime and reversing direction may be just as painful as the coming collapse will be. That is why time is short and transitional steps need to be taken if any attempt is going to be made at a somewhat smoother transition into the new. The new is coming one way or the other as the current system is unsustainable. The only question remains is whether we will be a part of fighting for a new system of Honest Money and Proper Government or whether we will be submitting to a One World New Order of the Ages under our would-be masters.

Before talking about how to transition let us continue to paint the picture of what we are transitioning too that was begun in Chapter 9 on "Debt Free Money". Remember Honest Money is not Printed Paper Currency. It is not lent into circulation by a central authority but is rather one or more of the commodities that rise up within a Free Market like any other but that fit certain attributes making it fit to be used as a Medium of Exchange. The use of which allows for the facilitating of trade, which increases wealth without producing Debt and consequently Debtors.

It was shown that employment and enterprise could be available to all who wish to contribute and participate. Additionally, how those wishing to take their leisure could do so without fear of loss simply by refraining from continually attempting to gain.

It was explained that a sufficient Supply of the Medium of Exchange (Money) to meet increased production would make real wealth available to ever increasing numbers without destroying the values of the production and labor of others.

Before these very attainable circumstances can come about it is incumbent on the People to wake up to the fraudulent nature of our current Debt Based Money, educate others and reject Fiat Money. All other political bickering needs to be set aside in recognition of the fact that the failure to correct this one major issue is a failure to correct almost any other by default. Any political figure that does not see the need for Congress to do its job and coin Money and set the Value thereof as a number one priority should not be elected to office.

To "Coin" is to stamp a piece of metal as to weight and fineness. To Regulate its Value is to operate on either Demand for, or the Supply of the metal the coin is stamped in. "Money" is metal such as Gold, Silver and Copper coined and issued to serve as a store of wealth, Medium of Exchange and a measure of Value. "Money" has value itself; Being a unit of wealth which automatically measures other value in terms of its own Intrinsic Value. "Currency" on the other hand is not Money it is Tokens, Government Notes and Bank Notes. "Notes" are promises to pay, IOU's, and without real "Money" in circulation "Notes" cannot be paid but only replaced with more "Notes". The only Paper that should be accepted as Money, if any, are Certificates of Deposits of Gold or Silver. This means a person holding one may go to a Bank or the issuer and receive the physical Gold or Silver they represent.

For Honest Money and the proper use of Gold and Silver as a Medium Congress must set a value equivalent to the existing standard of weights and measures. For example, if the term "Dollar" is to be used as a standard to measure "Value" then just as the term "Yard" is used to measure length it must remain a set standard. Just as a "Yard" has always consisted of three feet and a foot of twelve inches and has not varied as a standard; the "Dollar" if used as the measure of Value must remain constant from that point on. Whether a certain number of grains, grams or ounces is established once pegged it needs to remain the measure of Value. Then we will finally have not only a standard measure of length, weight and volume but also of Value.

Once this is done then the actual Value in goods, services and possessions can be measured in a unit which will record a true and accurate relationship between all wealth, whether rendered in Service, or represented by Goods and Possessions. Although the "Dollar", if used as the term for standard Value, would be pegged to a specific quantity or weight of Gold both Gold and Silver would function together. Even Copper or other acceptable elements may serve the lesser increments of exchange such as pennies to the dollar bill today.

Once a standard is set a system of answering the added Demand for Money in Gold must be established as previously stated to meet the goal of maintaining stable Prices and Value of goods and labor even as production increases and conversely should production and Demand decrease. To prevent any group or Nation from attempting to manipulate or monopolize the Market by corralling the Gold Supply or to prevent a problem due to a temporary or sudden change in the circumstances of the Supply and Demand of Gold, Silver would be used as a stabilizer. Just as coal, oil and natural gas can be used as an offset or market re-stabilizer for a sudden change in Supply and Demand for one energy source over another so Silver or other valuables can be used in a scientific manner or formula to offset any sudden Demands for Gold. By monetizing sufficient quantities of Silver whose value was measured in terms of Gold, the one standard, the Money Supply can be maintained at all times even with gold equivalents.

Bu maintaining a monitor on GDP (Gross Domestic Product) and a certain basket of commodities making up a proper CPI (Consumer Price Index) this pulse on the economy can be used as an indicator of when and by how much to adjust, the now one single lever, the Money Supply. This one lever in the hands of the People only via their directly elected representatives in Congress. With only one lever and one hand the chaos of today would be eliminated and blame for an improper adjustment easily determined. Any adjustment necessary, easily determined as the lever only can be pushed forward, increasing Money Supply, pulled back decreasing Supply or left alone in place. Child's play! Too far forward would show up in slight Price Inflation and too far back in Deflation the sweet spot of equilibrium being steadily holding Prices and Value.

With Debt Free Honest Money even the worst adjustment of the lever would amount to a stalled increase in the accumulation of wealth and a slowdown in the numbers rising above poverty or at the other extreme an overheated economy with increasing Inflation. Either of these occurrences making it totally apparent in which direction the lever would need to be adjusted for correction.

Gold and Silver being among the Natural Resources of the People, would thus require the People's and Government's portion from any mining operations, to be delivered to the Treasury for storage and coining into Money. That portion of which was retained for the Management and Laborers of the mining industry could be sold for the other industrial uses of Gold and Silver such as that used in electronics and jewelry, be deposited with the Treasury in exchange for Certificates of Deposit or minted into coin for their own use.

Government's Budget being a specific formula tied to GDP (Gross Domestic Product) and a percentage of the Increase of the People's wealth as reflected in Tax

Collection as well as a portion of the Imposts, Duties and percentages of other Natural Resource shares, the excess of which would add to the Treasury. The Treasury using these formulas along with the CPI (Consumer Price Index) would monetize amounts of Gold and Silver Coin and Certificates of Deposit used to pay Government obligations.

The Supply of Money in circulation monitored and regulated according to the stated goals of Government, to protect property by maintaining steady Prices and Labor and Property Values. Should indications of over-Supply present themselves, such as in an increasing CPI, the Treasury would refrain from the issuance of additional coinage or Certificates into circulation. Conversely if under-Supply presented itself, such as in falling CPI and GDP, then additional introduction of coin into circulation would be commenced. This could be accomplished by any of several means or a combination of some or all of them. Such actions as one-time expenditures by administration on civil infrastructure projects like dams or power production or a one-time across the board reduction or discount in the Income Tax for a given year among other ideas.

Prices of some individual commodities would fluctuate as this is the Markets way of fixing the Supply to the Demand. By having a fixed yardstick (Money of regulated value) it will show how much the change is and that the change is due to a change in the circumstances of Supply and Demand of that commodity itself, and not in the yardstick (the Value of Money).

Now this may all seem too simplistic and too Utopian to be true but the founding of this Nation on Honest Money and sound Government Principles led to the greatest, wealthiest and most free Nation the world has ever known. America in its early years with no Income Tax and no Central Banks had Budget Surpluses, no Debts and the most prosperity ever known along with Freedom and Liberty never experienced in the history of Governments.

Gradually, however, we began to modify our national government through the appointment of boards and commissions and the creation of various governmental agencies that made it impossible for the government to function in accordance with its Constitution. Finally, our real downward spiral began after the treasonous acts of those who handed away the Money Press with the Federal Reserve Act in December of 1913.

So, the Principles of Honest Money and Government although not very complicated to grasp and understand once brought to the light of day will be much harder to institute in light of the vast Power and Riches and Resources the enemy has accumulated during our confusion and sleep. These powerful interests which have made the present system yield them billions and billions of fraudulently gained profits are not going to just let the People or their Congress change that system without a fight.

The fight for the abolishing of the Federal Reserve, Fiat Money and un-Constitutional Government and Tax Collection has been being fought for years now by many brave Patriots who have lost fortune and family and have served Federal Prison sentences because of their efforts to win back out liberties and prolong the few remaining. You have never seen or heard of it in our mainstream News Media because they are owned and controlled by those reaping the billions from our current system.

Having exposed the Current System and set a vision for an honest one how do we get from here to there? Before answering the question of transition from one system to another let us look at Gold and Silver as a Medium of Exchange which few today have seen or held. Gold and Silver Coins are still produced today by Governments, Private Companies and certain Banks despite the disconnect of Currencies from the Gold Standard.

Some coins today along with other older ones no longer produced or of governments long past are traded and held by collectors for their beauty, value or history. These would be among those referred to as numismatics. "Numismatics" is the study or collection of monetary objects. Dealing in these require a certain knowledge as their values are not based solely on the amount of their gold content but also on their rareness or availability as well as their condition. Like all collector's items the desirability is in the eye of the beholder and can make arriving at a mutually agreed on value difficult which tends to limit the number of options available for transacting business.

For the novice or beginner in dealing with Gold and Silver or for its purposes in general commerce I suggest gold and silver bullion. "Bullion" is defined as bars and ingots but include non-numismatic coins. The simplicity is in the fact that their Price is a direct relation to the value of Gold or Silver and the content or amount of it in a given bar or coin.

Most of today's coins mark on their face the amount in weight and fineness of the metal they contain. Such as one ounce 0.999 find Gold or Silver. For those not so marked charts and books list the common coins and their content. Computing their value, a simple task of multiplying the gold or silver content and comparing it to current Spot Price found daily in every major newspaper or on any financial news station. "Spot Price" simply referring to the current cash Price per ounce. For example, if you wanted to buy a one-ounce Gold American Eagle coin you would simply find current Spot Price for Gold. If it were say $1,200 per ounce then you would know the current value of that bullion coin. Or if looking for a half ounce or tenth ounce coin you would divide accordingly.

Now it should be noted here that when dealing with today's coin dealers, depending on if you are buying from them or selling to them will determine actual Price. Although the current bullion coins are not numismatic some are more or less desirable due to design or country and therefore may vary some in premium. Premium being that fee the dealer tacks on to have a profitable business. For instance, you may find a dealer selling and American Eagle for Spot Price plus three percent or a Canadian Maple Leaf for Spot Price plus two percent. Meaning based on a Spot Price of $1,200 that you would pay $1,236 for the Eagle or $1,224 for the Maple Leaf. On the other hand, if you are selling to the Dealer you may find him only offering you Spot Price less two percent for the Eagle and Spot Price less three percent for the Maple Leaf being $1,176 and $1,164 respectively.

Various Countries produce various size coins of various fineness, but it is all simple math. For instance, the Mexican Peso is usually a coin of 1.25 ounces of Gold content which means you would just multiply Spot Price by 1.25 in this case getting $1,500. Below are some pictures of various gold and silver bullion coins and bars you may see.

As you can see from the above the artwork and symbols associated with the various pieces may be more or less desirable lending to some being used for more common everyday commerce and others to storage as possible future numismatics. You should know if you plan to save a piece for the future possibility of it being a collector's item that the least circulated the more desirable. Uncirculated and unscratched commanding the best Prices. Some dealers are selling them enclosed in plastic from the start for those who want to promote the condition and claim of an uncirculated piece.

Going along with percentage fineness marked on coins is the Karat markings on Gold Jewelry. The common markings of 10, 14, 18 and 24KT (Karat) on various pieces of jewelry is a system of designating its fineness in parts Gold to whatever other metal it is mixed with. Gold of 24 Karats is 0.999 percent fine, however, jewelry of this fineness is rare because Pure Gold is a relatively soft metal and would find itself easily dented, scratched or misshaped. Therefore, other metals are mixed in for durability. This means 14KT Gold is 14 parts Gold and 10 parts other.

To determine the value of its gold content alone you would take its total weight and multiply it by 14/24 or 0.583 to get the Gold portion. For example, a one ounce 14KT Gold chain with a Spot Price for Gold at $1,200 would have one ounce times 0.583, its content of Gold, multiplied by $1,200 to come up with $699.60 as the current value of the bullion Gold in the chain.

In an economy with gold and silver bullion coin being used to transact business we would quickly become as used to associating a gallon of milk, a pair of shoes or the purchase of a car with ounces of Gold or Silver as we currently are with Dollar bills. By tying the term "Dollar" to a specific unchanging weight of Gold the terms could be used interchangeably with real meaning.

CHAPTER 12

Transition

How do we transition from the current economic system to an Honest one? Can it be done without causing the nightmare that is approaching to arrive even sooner? You can be sure that when the scales fall off enough eyes for the clamor of change to be heard in the arena of public opinion that the Powers that be will do all in their power to discredit those promoting Honest Money.

When the movement is small, they will deride the ideas as foolish and hardly worth the consideration of intelligent people. Next, they will assassinate the character of promoters in an effort to keep the discussion on anything other than the facts and issues at hand. Eventuality they will use the levers they continue to hold to throw the system into additional chaos or disaster causing as much pain and misery as they can. Casting blame in an effort to shake the confidence of the People in the choices they are making. If the People keep their resolve however, the enemies ship will begin to break up with many of their own jumping overboard and swimming for the lifeboats of cooperation in hopes of avoiding criminal charges as more and more of their crimes come to light.

It is a principle of American Jurisprudence that fraud vitiates everything it's involved with. In other words, a party having been enticed into entering a contractual agreement by fraudulent means is not bound to the agreement in any of its terms. A person giving testimony under oath that is discovered to have lied in one point is to be given no benefit in the veracity of his other statements accompanying them. The ramifications of this when considering our vast National Debt, the millions of home mortgages and huge extension of loaned Credit is staggering.

When we consider that the loaning into circulation of Paper Money, let alone Credit from nothing, has been shown to be a fraud this actually makes every instrument and agreement associated with the list above able to be repudiated by any and all of their participants. The ramifications of which are mind boggling. The chaos of which would cause the unjust enrichment of some and the impoverishment of many others. This would be no more just for some than that which occurs under the current corruption.

Since chaos, pain, misery and poverty are what we are looking to overcome at the same time as we bring about opportunity, wealth, leisure and liberty we must attempt as orderly a transition as possible. The establishment of an Honest Money and an adequate Supply of it must come about at a rate equal to or as close to equal as conceivable to that of the rate at which dishonest Paper Money and loaned Credit are diminished.

Putting aside for a moment the things that could or

should be done to win the agreement of those necessary to bring about such a transition let us consider the transition itself.

To think that such a transition will be painless is to not grasp the extent of the corruption that has taken place to date or our own guilt in going along with placing such a burden of debt upon our children and grandchildren. Whether knowingly or ignorantly all participate in the effort to get ahead, of others, and few have dissented. After reading to this point in this book you are now among the knowingly. Being among the knowing places a burden of responsibility on you to either become a dissenter and participant in the battle for Honesty and Integrity, a minion of the enemy or a poltroonic fence sitter. Our posterity will most certainly place us in one of these categories.

Certainly, most of the pain and any injustice to occur should be borne by those most responsible for our current dilemma first, those who actively took advantage second and lastly all who went along to get along. These include the International Banker Money Men, Traitorous Politicians, the large Financial Firms and other Multi-Nationals. By right all their assets should be confiscated and debts owed to them repudiated as a result of their active participation in fraud. But for the sake of an orderly transition and to maintain a pressure for coopera-tion they must be left with some hope for themselves beyond bankruptcy and prison. But in issues where a short straw is to be drawn it is for them to be the holder.

It is in the very different and opposing attributes of

each Money type that just may allow for a somewhat orderly transition from one system to the other. Durable Intrinsically Valued Gold and Silver can remain in circulation indefinitely going from one hand to another repeatedly allowing for continuous transactions on a much smaller ratio of goods to Money Supply. Conversely Paper Money and Credit Extension out of thin air coupled with usury Interest Rates cause the Money Supply to shrink rapidly and disappear if not continuously increased and perpetuated.

Therefore, to cease Printing un-redeemable Paper Money and Extending Credit out of nothing is to shrink the "Fiat Money" out of existence. Since every bit of it in circulation was placed there by virtue of it being loaned to someone all of it is needed to pay back the loans and then some, that does not even exist, to pay the interest on those same loans. So, if just the act of paying back all loans will make the "Fiat Money Supply" disappear, after ceasing to allow creation of anymore, then how will the loan interest get paid and what will people use as a "Medium of Exchange"?

The loan interest itself is the most fraudulent part of the scheme of Fiat Money. As stated previously the contract itself for both the Principle and the Interest should be voidable due to fraud being present at all. But in the interest of keeping order and not rewarding borrowers and those overextended above those who live within their means without borrowing; I would propose an across-the-board reduction in interest rates to some maximum amount of just a few percent. Repayment of the Principle would return what was borrowed and serve to extinguish a corrupt Money Supply. The reduction of the interest rates would take away the Bankers fraudulent gains. The few percent allowed to remain would serve to pay employees and the cost of administration and settlement of the old system.

The allowance of any interest rate at all would mean that after the Fiat Money all disappeared by paying the Principle Loan Amounts back there would be some loan balance remaining. This remaining balance would have to come from the New Money Supply and would as stated pay Bank employees for their administration of closing the Old and transitioning to the New and for ongoing functions of proper banking described previously in an earlier chapter. The New Intrinsically Valued Money of Gold, Silver and equivalents such as Certificates of Gold and Silver Deposits would need to be introduced into circulation at a rate necessary to fill the gap being left by disappearing Fiat Money.

A date would need to be set that would indicate the line of demarcation for Old and New contracts. New Contracts would be allowed to demand payment in Real Money while Old Contracts would continue to be required to accept the Fiat (legal tender) Money as payment as long as it continued to exist. This would have an offsetting effect on the otherwise devalued currency. A currency soon to be discontinued would normally drop rapidly in value leaving holders of it with greatly devalued wealth. But in this case due to the rapidly disappearing nature of loaned Money and Credit the short Supply and preference of debtors wanting to pay their Old Debts with Fiat Money rather than the New Intrinsically Valued Gold or Silver would have the effect of propping up its value.

Although certain black-market stashes of cash from drug money, tax evaders and nervous foreigners would come on the scene at a large discount in exchange for New Money there would be no shortage of takers who preferred paying off their mortgages, credit cards and other loans with worthless Paper Money rather than valuable Gold and Silver. Any greater than estimated drop in value would be meaningless to the Debtors making payments as it would still be required to be accepted on Old Contracts. This ultimately would make the Bankers who issued it in the first place the loss takers at the end of the line, which is only right.

Some may argue that the announcement of a discontinuance of the current Money would lead to its abandonment by Foreign Governments and Investors and cause a huge repatriation or influx into this country causing runaway inflation. Foreigners would attempt to buy real goods and services from Americans and their Companies in an effort to exchange the perceived worthless paper for actual things and cause a huge rise in Price on everything. Although this may be true of a devalued currency if the currency itself was to remain the Medium of Exchange of the issuing Country or if there were a date on which the Currency would no longer be valid.

In this situation neither of these things are the case.

Although a date would be set for the start of the New Money, a date after which New Contracts could require only New Money payments, and a date after which Fiat Money and Credit would no longer be legal to create and issue, a date for the discontinued use of the Old Money would not be set. The reason no such date would be set or even need to be set is due to the attributes of Money loaned into circulation, when no longer created and issued it naturally disappears.

Consider that just before the date for New Money and discontinued issue of the Old a person takes out a 30-year mortgage on a home. That person now holds a contract allowing him to pay his mortgage in monthly payments over a 30-year period. Having entered into this agreement before the date representing the line of demarcation between the Old and New, he maintains the right to make payments on this Old Contract in Old Money, provided any remains. If indeed the "rapidly devalued and huge influx of Old Money" opinion is correct, then this mortgage payer would want to use his New Money to buy a large amount of this devalued Old Money so he could pay off his mortgage for pennies on the dollar with Old Money required to be accepted on Old Contracts.

This desire by the payers of Old Debt will remain until all Old Debt is paid and this demand will cause the Old Money to hold its value because by its very nature there is less of it in existence than there is Old Debt. At some point all Old Money will be used up paying off Old Debt and additional Debt will remain. Then New Money will be the only payment alternative. This fact will also prevent the shrinking Supply of the Old Money from becoming too highly valued because should its rarity cause its price to exceed that of the New Money debtors will just pay with the New Money and forgo the Old. This essentially will cap the Old at the value of the New, dollar for dollar.

This does not mean that foreigners not having dollar debts will not be dumping the Old Money they may very well want to be rid of it quickly. It will just mean that there will be takers for it here just as quickly. If the method of their abandonment is to buy American Goods and Services in exchange for this no longer desirable paper it will serve to increase American Businesses and lessen unemployment. This increased revenue will benefit government tax collection and aid it in extinguishing of Government Bond Obligations. The interest on Old Bond Obligations would be paid in Old Money essentially recycling the Money Foreign Bond Holders are abandoning back to them to abandon again until US Obligations are exhausted at which time the remaining Federal Reserve Notes (Old Money) would be returned to the Federal Reserve Banks to extinguish their US Bond Holdings.

Due to the nature of the Beast, the fact that even all Federal Reserve Notes are back in the Federal Reserve Banks hands debt will remain, because the interest due on them was never printed, at that point the remaining Debt will be repudiated. This will cancel the remaining National Debt and be a slap on the hand penalty for the

Federal Reserve Banks in comparison to the fraud and suffering they have reeked for over a century.

This virtual pardon being the bribe necessary to create an incentive for a peaceful and somewhat cooperative transition. If the Bankers are allowed a light at the end of the tunnel, over certain collapse and criminal indictment it should tend towards a decision to live and cheat another day. With the incentive of being able to mitigate some of the losses they are about to sustain and offered a part in the administration of proper banking functions with the New Honest Money the use of their current infrastructure would go a long way to an orderly transition.

It would be essential that Congress, before establishing the Standard Value Measurement of some weight of Gold or of Silver as the equivalent of some Dollar amount undertake to estimate the approximate existing quantity of Federal Reserve Notes. A census or survey of the quantities of Gold and Silver currently held by Government, the Federal Reserve Banks and the current production and potential Mining Operations in the Country would also be needed. This would aid them in estimating the available quantities and divisions needed and available to be created into a New Money Supply representing the Old.

Remember the use of the term Dollar as a standard of value for Money is only to aid in our understanding and our ease of comparing the cost of an item in today's so-called "Dollars" with the New actual Dollar (some particular weight of Gold or Silver). Nothing prevents the New System from abandoning the term Dollar altogether by just having people get used to an item costing an ounce of Gold or a half ounce, quarter ounce, etc.. the same with Silvers and Coppers. But for ease of transition being able to name items in current values would probably be preferable for most. Even if a Dollar's worth of Gold or Silver might be the size of a dime or less considering that Gold as of this writing is about 1,800 Federal Reserve Notes (dollars) per one ounce of Gold and my guess is that it is undervalued.

This is not to say that ones, fives, twenties etc.. very similar to what we use today as Federal Reserve Notes could not be produced for use. Only the New would not be notes (IOU's) but Certificates of Deposit each representing actual amounts of Gold or Silver that could be picked up by the bearer at any Depository (Bank or Government). This monitored by government with strict criminal penalties for fraud of any kind.

The more accurate the estimates of the Supply of Gold and Silver for use in monetizing into a Medium of Exchange (Money) made by Congress in their initial setting of the measurement of a Dollar in Gold weight the better for all. However, should those surveyed perjure themselves in their initial replies, future monitoring procedures should bring it to light. Additionally, either the over or under reporting will work to their detriment in the long run due to the nature of the New Honest Money System.

Since the initial survey is to establish a proper Dollar to weight equivalent based on available Supply of the commodities to be used in the making of Money, and the subsequent regulating of a sufficient supply for the transactions of the People, the stability of economy comes from the regulated supply. For Congress to overestimate the Supply would tend to have it set the Dollar per ounce standard value too low and to underestimate the Supply would tend to setting the Dollar per ounce too high. To overestimate the Supply and set the standard too low could certainly lead to future problems of not enough Supply for Demand. But this problem is easily eradicated by verification. In other words, if I say I have ten ounces I can show you ten ounces and so long as you check you cannot overestimate. The other side of the equation is more difficult because if I say I have ten ounces but really have fifteen you cannot verify more than the ten I show.

So, from the above you can see that the only inaccuracy that should occur is on the under estimating side of the equation. Under the New System this is not a problem for the System as much as it is for the under reporter. The under reporter in addition to risking future criminal indictment if discovered also ties up his reserve of under reported Gold or Silver store. This because the Government as the monetizer of coined Money and the verifier of Certificates of Deposit will preclude the ability of the under reporter from having the instruments representative of that store to use in the financial arena. In other words what good is it to a Banker to have hidden gold bars that he cannot loan against or otherwise use as Money in the financial business that he is in? It would be wasted Capital. Yes, he could probably find a way to sell it for its value but that would be a onetime gain far less detrimental to society as a whole than what occurs today. The continued use of it to produce income by having initially monetized it would be far more beneficial to him.

With regard to the System this underestimate has little effect. It just means more will be available eventually for monetizing if needed, far less a problem then having over estimated and then being without it. The sudden additional Supply as a commodity will not cause Price changes of other commodities as the Government regulates Money Supply and will not monetize it before it's needed as an addition to the Supply of a Medium of Exchange.

In simple terms let us say there is one source of Gold for Money and Congress estimates it to be 100 ounces and they then estimate existing Federal Reserve Notes at $2,000. This would mean to have Gold be a replacement to represent the value that the $2,000 Federal Reserve Notes currently represent they would set the Dollar equivalent to $20 per ounce of Gold. (20 x 100 ounces = 2,000) If it were discovered that in fact only 80 ounces were actually available this would be a problem if they could only coin less that would mean they decreased the Money Supply or if they had issued Certificates of Deposit redeemable in actual Gold it would mean they didn't have enough Gold to cover redemption.

Therefore, verification is necessary. On the reverse side should it be discovered that 110 ounces existed while only 100 were coined or issued against, this would not cause a problem as full redemption is easily covered and that which is issued served as a full divisional value for all Federal Reserve Notes they replaced. The additional 10 ounces will simply not be coined or monetized until such a time that expanded wealth and economic monitors (CPI & GDP) call for it.

This will give all Banks and Bankers along with anyone else with large stores of Gold and Silver who want a place in the financial arena to properly self-report. They will want their store coined for them for a small fee or they will want the verifiable Certificates of Deposit for financial dealings.

Now I am sure some purists will argue that Certificates of Deposit should not exist in the New Money Supply and that only coined Gold and Silver itself should be used. The argument would be that Certificates of Deposit even though redeemable for actual Gold or Silver would go largely unredeemed, the people being happy to just pass around the Certificates themselves. This would lead once again to Bankers and Politicians getting the bright idea to issue more Certificates than can physically be redeemed while assuming it will never happen. Essentially returning to Fractional Reserve Banking. I do not totally disagree with them such an assumption or fear is more than warranted. History itself almost assures it.

My reason for proposing otherwise is that we have a real uphill battle in overcoming the current corruption as it is. Without the eventual support of the majority, it may never happen. The less inconvenience and interruption in the People's current habits the easier the sell. If they only need to be sold on the soundness of a concept, they may get behind it but calling all to specific action and fully changed habits maybe an impossible task. Once accomplished it will be for those who know the ongoing danger of corruption to act and make sure sound systems of verification are in place. Additionally, it will be incumbent on us to teach and educate each generation in our schools about the Principles of Sound Money, Sound Government and the terrible History that will repeat itself if not adhered to.

By design the Reserve Bankers will know that once they are the holders of all Federal Reserve Notes at the end of the line, and the only remaining holders of our National Debt, that the remainder will be repudiated (canceled). At first glance this may seem a disincentive to their reluctant cooperation. But as shown with the removal of the incentive to hide stores of Gold and the desire of all still holding Old Debt to obtain Federal Reserve Notes, to pay with it; the incentive for the Reserve Bankers will be to gather their notes back in not re-release them.

Because of the incentive for Debtors to pay Old Debts with Old Money illegal re-issuance would be detrimental to their financial position. Because Debtors would gladly gobble it up to pay not only the Principle amounts but the remaining Administrative Interest Rate portion that was allowed to remain. In other words, if the Banks don't work to gather up all the outstanding Federal Reserve Notes all Old Debts will be paid off with their own now worthless paper. The sooner the Federal Reserve Notes are out of circulation the sooner remaining Debt balances will need to be paid in New Money bringing them New System Profits. This may even serve as an incentive for Banks to use gold reserves to buy up large quantities of Old Money in order to retire it.

Change in the Tax Code would be made as previously discussed in an earlier chapter. They would occur on the same date of demarcation between the Old and New Money issuance. Income would be computed on your gains from both New and Old Money under the New Rules but be payable in either, until the Old is exhausted. This would not matter to the Government as they would re-spend either until all Bond Interest on Government Obligations were paid to foreign governments and individual investors. After this they would drain circulation of any they received and destroy it or make final payment on the National Debt to Reserve Banks with the remainder, if any.

The pessimism and cynicism that pervade today's political and economic climate may dampen the ability of the majority to believe the possibility or envision the prosperity and liberty that would be the sure result of Honest Money and Proper Government. But dramatic change is never brought about by majorities it begins with courageous individuals who act on their beliefs.

Although fading fast the Greatness of this Country and its liberties that remain are the remnants of a few visionaries who acted. They declared independence, fought for liberty and instituted Honest Money and

Constitutional Government. That vision and action became the greatest, richest, most free and powerful nation on earth in the history of man. Enemies have been against it since its inception, and they finally have us down on one knee the question is whether they will succeed in toppling her over or will a few brave and courageous individuals act and help her to her feet again?

CHAPTER 13

What Can You Do

The controlled News Media, Corrupt Central Bankers and Treacherous Politicians will not go near the topic of Fiat Money verses Honest Money to save their souls. Although they talk constantly about the economy and financial markets as though it's their main concern you will never hear them address Money itself. What Money is and what it's for and how it enters circulation is never addressed as having optional considerations. Money is taken for granted to be a set thing and contemplating anything other than what we know it to be is as silly as trying to replace the wheel as an idea.

But as you have discovered, this is an illusion, a slight of hand by the guilty, "Pay no attention to the man behind that curtain", says the great and powerful Oz. So, "What can you do?", becomes the question. "What difference can I make?", you may ask. If the News Media will not cover it and politicians will not discuss it, how will we ever reach critical mass? If few people can even agree on the problem how will change ever come about?

There will be numerous opinions on how best to raise awareness and to finally get the real issues into the Public Spotlight. Which one is best? If there is a best way, it will finally come to the forefront by its virtue of actually having been the best. Do we need to know ahead of time what it is? I don't believe so! My opinion on the best method is this: that everyone who has an opinion as to what would be the best way should themselves champion that way and get those they can convince to join them.

Taking the knowledge and understanding that has been gained and going back to being apathetic or feeling defeated by the scope of the problem is not the answer. It is true that the problem itself is the cause of many who suffer from lack of time and money to do anything about it. In other words, the problem it causes perpetuate the inability of many to fight against it.

Certainly, it will always be that some do more and others less. But certainly, all that are concerned and become aware can do something. Even if that something is buying a copy of this book to give to someone else or simply suggesting it be bought. Raising the consciousness and awareness of one more person is doing something. Who knows it may just turn out to be the person who makes all the difference in the world?

Writing politicians, sending your local congress person a copy or simply asking them a hard question about these topics in front of others when they are out campaigning for your vote. Let them know the only politicians you plan on voting for are ones who think that this is the most pressing issue. Let them know when the next financial disaster comes you are not going to let them escape the fact that they were aware of all the issues and dangers and refused to act.

As stated previously change is not a matter of if but of when and how painful. Dishonest Money cannot be sustained without worse and worse consequences at each bust after each boom. The web is getting so tangled they can no longer handle the levers of control no matter how ignorant the People remain. Huge upheavals and upsets are in everyone's future if a proper transition is not begun soon. I am not a doomsday advocate nor a pessimist in fact I may be considered an optimist, romanticist or even a dreamer by those aware of the facts for even believing a transition is possible. I'd like to think I am a realist and doing my small part not to be placed by our posterity in the category of an apathetic and spineless fence sitter or worse, when history is written.

The consequences of doing nothing are very real. Today poverty exists in the midst of plenty. More food goes to waste daily than the worlds hungry could eat. We have more millionaires and billionaires than ever in history. Yet we still have unemployment, homelessness and hunger. The misery and suffering of real souls occur all over the world and the number one and two causes are corrupt Money and corrupt Government no other reasons come close to these two. The Scriptures site the top two reasons for the top two causes of the problem. One is that the love of Money is the root of all evil. This it calls idolatry. The other is the failure of the People to obey the commands of the Almighty. This is summed up by not doing unto others as you would have them do unto you.

This concurs with my earlier observation that our circumstances are the result of not only the actions of the perpetrators but our actions in response. As I write this India is in the News. The "Economist" magazine has no less than three articles, the Wall Street Journal and certain major news stations have reported in days past about its government's decision on monetary reform. You may recall in an earlier chapter how I gave an example of the possibility of a government suddenly changing from Green Paper to say Red Paper Money instead. I mentioned how the Green suddenly being worthless could not buy anything but if you held Gold as savings, it could easily have been exchanged for some amount of the new Red Money. Did you think that was a far fetched example? Did you take even a minute to imagine your circumstances or position if it were to occur that day? Probably not! But here we are a short spell later this book not even complete and the People of India are in the middle of huge problems, loss and suffering.

What India's Government is totting as a move against the Black Market and Tax Evaders is currently causing widespread misery and suffering for everyone. Most likely the least of which are the rich, the black market or the tax evaders. Their President Norendra Modi announced that all 500 and 1,000 Rupee Notes were being pulled from circulation and that small business acceptance of them was now illegal. Everyone holding them could turn them into the Central Bank by year end (less than 60 days) for Bank Credit or replacement by 500 and 2,000 Rupee Notes. The problem being the new notes will take five to six months to print enough to replace what has been canceled. Fear is large amounts turned into the Bank will be questioned and compared against past tax payments and penalties assessed.

This action is leading to all the classic symptoms outlined in earlier chapters. The sudden loss of a sufficient Supply of the Medium of Exchange is shutting down businesses, putting workers out of work, collapsing Prices and leaving produce in the fields to spoil. Now lest you think it can't happen elsewhere then while searching and reading about this incident also search Burma 1987, Soviet Union 1991, North Korea 2009 and don't forget the Great Depression USA.

As long as people accept IOU's that are never paid as payment for their goods and labor they will remain at the mercy of Bankers and Politicians for their very lives. If you have lived or been in the Northeast during a large snowstorm you should have some idea about how fast the store shelves can be emptied of goods. Be assured that snowstorms are only one of many occurrences that can produce those same effects. By all means rely on the Almighty above all for your needs but also use the brain you were given and the wisdom you obtain as you go. Be prepared to provide for yourself and your own by demanding payment in real Money or Value in exchange for your precious time, labor and goods.

At the very least 20 to 30% percent of your savings should be in Gold or Silver. As shown previously this could serve to replace the loss of all your Paper Dollars or Electronic Credits should the need arise and it's going to if something doesn't change soon. Those in India of this mindset are sitting pretty compared to their neighbors who are relying on Government and Bankers to do something. Oh, in case you haven't thought about it, you cannot eat or drink Gold or Silver either. So be sure to use some of that worthless Paper while people are still accepting it to handle both those needs for longer than three days also.

Remember the Debtor is Slave to the Lender. In my opinion it is better to be flat broke than to be in Debt. Think of all the time you have spent paying interest. Think of all the things you bought that you couldn't resell even a week later for as much as you paid for it. The VCR with four heads or the TV with picture in a picture and all the other items bought on Credit against time payments. Overpaid for to have the privilege of paying later rather than now. Would you have made a different choice if cash on the spot was demanded? What if Gold or Silver were required? What if the items were priced by the number of hours or weeks you'd be at work paying for them? You do love your job, right? Is that why you let them pay you Paper IOU's?

I'm not trying to make anyone feel angry, foolish or depressed at least not with themselves. But I am trying to make you feel something because emotion makes people act. Apathy, ignorance and carelessness does not make for change but neither does it make for escaping the consequences of not changing anything. Yes, we are each only one person and even all together behind one opinion about the best action to take may not win the day anytime soon. But certainly, you can put yourself and those close to you in a better position to weather the storms. Being able to have someone else to blame will not change the experience you go through.

The principles of Sound Money and Sound Government need to be taught to as many as will listen and most especially to the next generation. Should collapse occur we need knowledgeable men and women to know what needs to replace the old. Getting courses and seminars together for businessmen and students both young and old is essential. These topics should be introduced in grade school, home school, college, Sunday school and at Boy Scouts and Girl Scouts.

Those currently in Debt should look for and follow plans to escape it. Start by paying off your smallest regular revolving debt payment first then as they drop off continue to think of that payment amount as still needing to be paid. Then by using the freed-up funds to add to the reduction of the next smallest and so on until all Debt is eliminated. You will be surprised how well and fast it can work. Next continue this habit even after Debt is cleared to build an emergency fund. This should be an amount of at least six months to a year of your income or expenses.

Once you reach this point you are ready to consider yourself a saver. Now without all kinds of monthly Debt payments you should be able to save no less than 10% percent of your income. Of that savings be sure you convert at least 20 to 30% percent of it to Gold and Silver and don't worry about the Price of Gold and Silver going up or down. If it goes down keep doing your regular purchasing of it and your average cost per ounce will also be getting less by virtue of "Dollar Cost Averaging". If the Price is rising, then your investment is appreciating. Up or down when economic upheavals do occur it will all shoot up quickly. If they do not occur, you will remain ready and your other 70 to 80% of savings will be doing fine keeping up with the Jones's in whatever popular investments your into.

For those that have success in the above plan I would suggest that if you also want Spiritual success and a great feeling save aside a second 10% percent of your income in an account and enjoy finding people in need and circumstances to give it away to. Give thanks daily for any blessings you can count and keep it all a secret!

After converting to gold and silver stop counting it in terms of Dollars and start thinking in terms of I have 10, 20, 30 or however many ounces of each built up. Remember it's not 1800 Federal Reserve Notes buys me an ounce of Gold but rather an ounce of Gold buys me 1800 Federal Reserve Notes or whatever the then current figure is. An ounce of Gold remains an ounce of Gold it doesn't do the changing. The value of the Federal Reserve Note is what changed. An ounce of Gold several years ago bought 300 Federal Reserve Notes and now it buys 1800 of them. The Federal Reserve Notes got cheaper or lost value not the Gold. Think of the loss being invested in Paper Money took over that period of time yet few people see it that way.

Remember Wealth is not a pile of the Medium of Exchange, especially when that Medium is Paper Currency or Electronic Credits. It is the things that Medium can buy. We accept worthless Paper as payment and use it to purchase things for no other reason than others also do it. Like my mom always asked, "if your friends jump off a bridge are you going to do that to"?

History testifies that what an ounce of Gold could buy yesterday it can still buy today. It also shows however, that what 300 Federal Reserve Notes could buy yesterday takes 1,800 of them today. So, which one will you use to store the representation of your labor for future spending?

It has been demonstrated that the only factor preventing a person genuinely willing to work from finding work or a person having goods to sell, that others desire to buy, from having them purchased is the insufficient Supply of a Medium of Exchange. Conceivably then if every time a dollars' worth of goods were produced and a dollars' worth of labor was expended a dollars' worth of Gold or Silver was coined for use in representing that labor and those goods there would be no reason a transaction could not occur.

Imagine a giant outdoor Marketplace set up on the land of some extremely wealthy man. Everybody that comes sets up tables and booths displaying all the goods they produced and brought to the Market to sell. Suddenly the rich landowner announces he will buy every good on every table and in every booth. His only condition is that all the Money he uses to buy the goods must be spent on the goods at his Marketplace. He further assures them that the Price of all goods will be the very same Price he paid for them. Do you think the owners of the goods at each table will agree to this proposal? Who do you think will be the happiest? Will they return again the following week?

I hope your answers to the above questions are yes you'd agree and yes you'd be back the following week. My guess is the happiest among them would be those that produced and brought the most goods to the Marketplace. Why? Because a Market like this would mean all the goods I produced were purchased. How much better can business be than to sell your whole inventory? The following week I might even try to bring more to the Market. And certainly, I am happy to use the Medium of Exchange I received to purchase the things I want at other tables and booths coming away with Wealth equal to that in value of the things that I produced to exchange for them. Even if the Market that week did not have a particular good I would prefer, knowing Prices remain very stable at this Market I could purchase a durable good that I could return with next time and then locate the preferred item. I could do the same for a very large expensive item by building up a collection of Gold or Silver rounds finally returning with enough to make the larger purchase.

Now imagine how happy and appreciative you would be if prior to going to the rich landowners Marketplace you had been going to the Big Bankers Marketplace where you brought your goods to Market but were never sure how much you would sell. Going away with half your goods still unsold you would spend the week no bothering to produce any more goods waiting to try again the following week. Not selling enough you find yourself borrowing Money from the Banker at interest to buy some of the things you need from other tables. They in turn doing the same. Then when repayment is due needing to give the Money from the few sales made to the Banker to keep him from taking the rest of your goods at half value to pay back. After experiencing the other would you ever come back to this one?

The above two imaginary Markets are certainly simplistic versions of an economy but the vast difference from one to the other is far from imaginary. Honest Money and Property Protective Government widens the middle class and reduces the super-rich as well as the extremely poor. Dishonest Money leads to corrupt Government, a Super Wealthy Elite class, a shrinking Middle class and burgeoning poverty.

Unfortunately, no matter how clear our understanding or how willing we are to help educate others, speak out against corruption, refer this book to others an economy that doesn't yet exist cannot be participated in. So, beside the above, reducing debt and setting aside gold and silver bullion as savings, What can you do?

Well how about getting together with other likeminded individuals and companies willing to exchange goods and labor for Honest Value. Nothing is stopping you from requesting payment for your goods and labor in ounces of Gold and or Silver bullion. Or likewise offering to pay for goods and services with ounces of Gold or Silver. Although currently there is no rich landowner of a Marketplace that will guarantee the purchases of all goods and labor you may be willing to bring to it there are other like-minded individuals willing to deal with each other in Honest Money and Honest exchange. And although this currently would require you to purchase some amount of Gold and or Silver bullion to have available to deal in, remember, unlike loaned paper, Gold and Silver does not disappear from circulation so the same bullion rounds or coins can go back and forth and around over and over again. This means a few ounces of either Gold or Silver can facilitate many times their value in transactions.

For example, let's say a certain landscaper mows the lawn and trims the hedges of a certain hardware store owner who pays him three ounces of Silver for the job. The landscaper takes these down to a certain farmer he knows and buys some produce and uses the same three ounces of Silver to pay for it. This farmer's tractor breaks, and he goes to the hardware store owner and uses the same three ounces of Silver to pay for the part. Next week when the lawn gets cut again guess what the hardware store owner uses to pay the landscaper. That's right the same three pieces of Silver.

This is the proper use of a Medium of Exchange to facilitate transactions and to serve as a store of value until your prior output (your labor) can come back to you by the saved Medium's future use. In our example the hardware store owner got his lawn cut twice for the same three Silver coins. The farmer fixed his tractor and the landscaper bought produce and is still now holding three coins. Not one of them is in debt to the other or to any Banker. All accounts are always square. If this was to go on for a year the hardware store owner would have had his lawn taken care of every week the landscaper would have groceries every week and the farmer would have the tools and parts he needed to yield the crops. All on the same Debt Free three pieces of Silver.

Now if the hardware store owner was the last one of this small group to be introduced to the idea of Honest Money and initially worried about how much Gold or Silver he would need to participate with the others that were doing business this way he soon discovered how to get 52 weeks of landscaping for three silver coins.

Before what I said above is misconstrued most certainly he paid the landscaper three coins each week for a total of 156 coins and if the hardware store owner had no goods or services to offer himself it would have cost him every one. But because he also had goods and services worth someone paying him three coins a week for he was able to participate by initially only needing to buy or save three aside to begin having a part with other like-minded people.

If you have fully grasped the implications of the corruption, we daily find ourselves a part of, originally out of ignorance and subsequently from lack of choice, you may wish to extract yourself by demanding payment in Gold or Silver and offering to make payment in them as well. If you have the luxury of this option that is wonderful but for most, I would imagine they would meet with resistance whether requesting such as payment or offering it as payment. With current legal tender laws and the majorities unfamiliarity regarding Gold and Silver as Money for most a sudden and complete change would be next to impossible.

Although you or your business may not be able to make such a change nothing prevents you from making it an option. Inquiries about such an option might be a great way to get the topic brought up for conversation. Maybe a sign stating discounts applied to payments in Gold or Silver would get you customers asking, "What is that about?" providing a great opportunity to enlighten the curious. You may be surprised by those that may take advantage of the discount. The sign could even mention the availability of this book to learn more or give one of the numerous web sites regarding the topic.

By slowly and steadily increasing the number of your customers or clients who pay in Honest Money while also locating suppliers and service providers who prefer receiving payments this way as well you could find yourself eventually totally independent of the economic worries of the general public. Boons and busts and inflation and recession periods could be meaningless to you and others in their own private economy.

Be sure to check out the Appendix at the back of this book for additional book titles related to this and other topics as well as the internet web sites listed for the various groups and barter sites as well as some dealers of Gold and Silver bullion. Also included is a discount coupon for bulk purchases of this book. Aquaregics, LLC (www.aquaregics.com) a carrier of gold and silver bullion pieces, among others, also has provided the readers of "What about Money" a coupon for a discount on its signature one ounce Gold Time Piece coin. This is an offer for one of my favorite Gold coins not only is it an ounce of Gold being offered at a price (1%) one percent below current Spot Price but it is a work of art. Aquaregics' Gold and Silver Time Piece Series and their depiction of the Time Pieces of History will make you want to have one of each for your own collection.

Most importantly I would like to urge you to visit and join the Foundation for a Debt Free Society. The Foundation is dedicated to the main principles outlined in this book and the goal of bringing about a Debt Free Society. On its web site you can find a host of information and links to various related topics, news and forums. Members can participate in their own Debt Free Society Marketplace buying, selling or trading in TrueNotes which are backed and redeemable in actual Gold and or Silver bullion. With escrow agent and payment verification services it is a great location to meet and deal with other like-minded individuals and companies. The support of this membership will aid you in building and more easily attracting others to your network locally. By having a place to refer those you introduce to the idea of Honest Money they can more quickly get information and obtain their own Gold and Silver bullion or at the least join and obtain any discount you may be offering for doing so. The address for FDFS is www.debtfreesociety.org.

Before closing I would like to say I am not usually an advocate of generalizations I try to judge each person by their own actions and character. In this writing I have used many adjectives in describing Bankers, Politicians, Government Administrators and others. My condemnation (which I make no apologies for in regard to those among these classes who are conscious of the choices they are making) is directed at those who could speak out or take action who don't and those who directly advocate for their own advantage over others. Certainly, I recognize many small bankers like the general population do not have a clue any more than most government workers who believe in conscientiously doing their jobs. I'd even like to believe a few politicians are genuinely civic minded and would advocate for Honest Money if they were aware there were options. So, with that said I hope no one will misconstrue my previous statements and likewise not paint all those in these positions with the same brush. Rather if you have access to some in these positions attempt to bring them to the light. You never know from where the tide may turn. May the Almighty fill you with the Spirit of Truth.

APPENDIX A

Glossary of Terms

Appreciation: is an increase in value

Bartering: to trade by exchanging one commodity for another: to trade goods or services in exchange for other goods or services

Black-market: illicit trade in goods or commodities in violation of official regulations
also: a place where such trade is carried on

Capital: relating to or being assets that add to the long-term net worth of a corporation; that portion of savings used as an initial investment into business or other ventures

Capital Expenditures: an amount paid out that creates a long-term benefit (as one lasting beyond the taxable year) especially: costs that are incurred in the acquisition or improvement of property (as capital assets) or that are otherwise chargeable to a capital account NOTE: Capital expenditures are not deductible for income tax purposes. They are generally added to the property's basis.

Capital Gain: the increase in value of an asset (such as stock or real estate) between the time it is bought and the time it is sold

Capitalism: an economic system characterized by private or corporate ownership of capital goods, by investments that are determined by private decision, and by prices, production, and the distribution of goods that are determined mainly by competition in a free market

Caveat Emptor: a principle in commerce: without a warranty the buyer takes the risk (Buyer Beware)

Commodities: an economic good: such as a product of agriculture or mining; agricultural commodities like grain and corn; an article of commerce especially when delivered for shipment

Communism: a system in which goods are owned in common and are available to all as needed; a theory advocating elimination of private property; a totalitarian system of government in which a single authoritarian party controls state-owned means of production

Compound Interest: interest computed on the sum of an original principal and accrued interest

Consumer Price Index: an index measuring the change in the cost of typical wage-earner purchases of goods and services expressed as a percentage of the cost of these same goods and services in some base period

<u>Corporate Taxes</u>: are just collectivist methods of hiding a greater tax burden. Corporations and all for profit businesses exist and function to create a profit. <u>ALL</u> Taxes and expenses including the cost of Regulation is and has to be passed on to the consumer in the price of the goods and services they pay for. If this in not done the business will not profit and therefore not continue. Therefore a 50% Tax Rate whether the individual is seen to pay 10% and the business 40% is nonetheless equal to the individual paying the whole 50%. The only difference being how much is called Tax and how much is called Price

<u>Corrupt</u>: to change from good to bad in morals, manners, or actions; to degrade with unsound principles or moral values

<u>Credit</u>: the balance in a person's favor in an account; an amount or sum placed at a person's disposal by a bank, corporation or other person

<u>Credit Money</u>: money accepted because of the credit of the issuer rather than for its intrinsic commodity value

<u>Credit Rating</u>: a score or grade that a company or organization gives to a possible borrower and that indicates how likely the borrower is to repay a loan

<u>Currencies</u>: something (such as coins, treasury notes, and banknotes) that is in circulation as a medium of exchange; paper money in circulation

<u>Debit</u>: an entry on the left-hand side of an account constituting an addition to an expense or asset account or a deduction from a revenue, net worth, or liability account

<u>Debt Based Money System</u>: a system that creates more and more debt characterized by loaning fiat currencies into circulation to serve as the medium of exchange

<u>Debt Instruments</u>: instruments such as IOU's, Federal Reserve Notes and others that trade in debt obligations

<u>Deflation</u>: an act or instance of deflating: the state of being deflated; a contraction in the volume of available money or credit that results in a general decline in prices

<u>Dejure</u>: by right: of right; based on laws or actions of the state

<u>Demand</u>: willingness and ability to purchase a commodity or service: the quantity of a commodity or service wanted at a specified price and time – supply and demand

<u>Democracy</u>: a government in which the supreme power is vested in the people and exercised by them directly or indirectly through a system of representation usually involving periodically held free elections – mob rule

<u>Depreciation</u>: to lower the price or estimated value of / / depreciate property: to deduct from taxable income a portion of the original cost of (a business asset) over several years as the value of the asset decreases

<u>Dollar</u>: a specific number of grains of silver or gold used to set a monetary value; since abandoned and now used as the name of US Currency (one Federal Reserve note)

<u>Earned Income Credit</u>: so-called credit paid to low income earners in the US Tax Code; a transfer tax which takes from single persons and high wage earners to give to low income filers

<u>Equilibrium</u>: a state of adjustment between opposing or divergent influences or elements; In a Free-Market prices rise and fall and find their equilibrium as previously explained due to Supply and Demand

<u>Evil</u>: is causing or threatening distress or harm it is also the fact or suffering, misfortune and distress and a source of sorrow, distress or calamity

<u>Federal Reserve Note</u>: a currency note issued by the Federal Reserve banks; a negotiable debt instrument; a promise to pay with a promise to pay

<u>Fiat</u>: a command or act of will that creates something without or as if without further effort; legal tender declared legal by government despite the lack of intrinsic value

<u>Fractional Reserves</u>: is a system in which only a fraction of bank deposits are backed by actual cash on hand and available for withdrawal

<u>Free Market</u>: is one where voluntary exchange and the laws of supply and demand provide the sole basis for the economic system, without government intervention

<u>Gold</u>: a yellow metallic element that occurs naturally in pure form and is used especially in coins, jewelry, and electronics

<u>Gold Standard</u>: a monetary standard under which the basic unit of currency is defined by a stated quantity of gold and which is usually characterized by the coinage and circulation of gold, unrestricted convertibility of other money into gold, and the free export and import of gold for settling of international obligations

<u>Gross Domestic Product</u>: the gross national product excluding the value of net income earned abroad

<u>Hedge</u>: to protect oneself from losing or failing by a counterbalancing action

<u>Income Taxes</u>: a tax on the net income of an individual or a business

<u>Inflation</u>: a continuing rise in the general price level usually attributed to an increase in the volume of money and credit relative to available goods and services; Specifically, an effect of increasing the Supply of Money in circulation

<u>Interest</u>: a charge for borrowed money generally a percentage of the amount borrowed; the profit in goods or money that is made on invested capital

Investment: the outlay of money usually for income or profit: capital outlay; also: the sum invested or the property purchased

Investor: a person who invests

IOU's: an I owe you receipt making a promise to pay

Legal Tender: money that is legally valid for the payment of debts and that must be accepted for that purpose when offered (as decreed by government)

Macrocosm: the great world: UNIVERSE; a complex that is a large-scale reproduction of one of its constituents

Maximum Credit Absorption: The point where current use of Credit cannot be expanded further; Where past and current Credit obligations absorb and exceed available Credit Extension.

Medium of Exchange: something commonly accepted in exchange for goods and services and recognized as representing a standard of value

Microcosm: a community or other unity that is an epitome of a larger unity; a greatly diminished size, form, or scale

Money: something generally accepted as a medium of exchange, a measure of value, or a means of payment

Money Supply: the total amount of money available in an economy for spending as calculated by any of various methods (as by adding total currency to funds available in private checking accounts)

Monopolize: to get a monopoly of: assume complete possession or control of

Numismatic: the study or collection of coins, tokens, and paper money and sometimes related objects (such as medals)

Open Market Operations: is an activity by a central bank to give (or take) liquidity in its currency to (or from) a bank or a group of banks

Ponzi Scheme: an investment swindle in which some early investors are paid off with money put up by later ones in order to encourage more and bigger risks

Promissory Note: a written promise to pay at a fixed or determinable future time a sum of money to a specified individual or to bearer

Republic: a government in which supreme power resides in a body of citizens entitled to vote and is exercised by elected officers and representatives responsible to them and governing according to law

Silver: a very malleable metallic chemical element with atomic number 47 that is capable of a high degree of polish, has the highest thermal and electric conductivity of any substance, and that is used especially in jewelry and tableware, in electronics, and as an antimicrobial

<u>Simple Interest</u>: interest paid or computed on the original principal only of a loan or on the amount of an account

<u>Socialism</u>: a system or condition of society in which the means of production are owned and controlled by the state; it is that phase of democracy which negates property rights and anarchy the phase which negates law

<u>Spot Price</u>: the price of spot goods—contrasted with future price

<u>Stock</u>: the proprietorship element in a corporation usually divided into shares and represented by transferable certificates

<u>Supply</u>: the quantity or amount (as of a commodity) needed or available

<u>Time Value of Money</u>: is a basic financial concept that holds that money in the present is worth more than the same sum of money to be received in the future

<u>Transfer Payments</u>: money (such as welfare payments) that is received by individuals and that is neither compensation for goods or services currently supplied nor income from investments (stealing from the rich to give to the poor)

<u>Transfer Tax</u>: a tax (as a gift tax or estate tax) imposed on the transfer of property

<u>Usury</u>: the lending of money with an interest charge for its use especially: the lending of money at exorbitant interest rates

<u>Velocity of Money</u>: is the frequency at which one unit of currency is used to purchase domestically-produced goods and services within a given time period. In other words, it is the number of times one dollar is spent to buy goods and services per unit of time

<u>Wealth Based Money System</u>: is one that wealth is produced all around for all based on an honestly valued commodity such as gold and/or silver being used as the Medium of Exchange

APPENDIX B

Reading Alternatives

"None Dare Call It Conspiracy" by Gary Allen

"The Creature from Jekyll Island: A Second Look at the Federal Reserve" by G. Edward Griffin

"THE ILLUMINATI: Secrets of a New World Order" by Phil Coleman

"The Law by Frederic Bastiat

"The Constitution of the United States of America: The Declaration of Independence, The Bill of Rights" by Founding Fathers

"The Tyranny of the Federal Reserve" by Brian O'Brien

"Billions For The Bankers – Debts For The People" by Mr. John Larry Flinchpaugh

"The Secrets of the Federal Reserve" by Eustace Mullins

"Bloodlines of the Illuminati" by Fritz Springmeier

"The Hardcore Prepper's Guide to Survival Bartering" by David Presnell

"The Lords of Easy Money: How the Federal Reserve Broke the American Economy" by Christopher Leonard

"A World of Lies Collusion and Conspiracy: And how to see past it" by Michael Ogden

"The Greatest Lie on Earth: Proof That Our World Is Not a Moving Globe" by Edward Hendrie

APPENDIX C

Internet Sites

Mortgage Calculators:

https://www.mortgagecalculator.org/

https://www.calculator.net/mortgage-calculator.html

https://www.nerdwallet.com/mortgages/mortgage-calculator

Time Value of Money:

https://www.thecalculator.co/finance/Time-Value-of-Money-Calculator-380.html

https://www.gigacalculator.com/calculators/time-value-of-money-calculator.php

https://online-calculator.org/time-value-of-money-calculator.aspx

Compound Interest:

https://www.gigacalculator.com/calculators/compound-interest-calculator.php

https://www.thecalculatorsite.com/finance/calculators/compoundinterestcalculator.php

Currency Exchange:

https://www.calculator.net/currency-calculator.html

https://fx-rate.net/calculator/

Debt Consolidation:

https://www.calculator.net/debt-consolidation-calculator.html

https://www.debt.org/consolidation/best-way-to-consolidate-debt/

https://www.debtfreesociety.org

https://whataboutmoney.org/

https://www.truenotes.org/

Gold & Silver:

https://www.aquaregics.com

https://silvergoldbull.com/

https://www.moneymetals.com/

https://www.jmbullion.com/

https://www.goldeneaglecoin.com/

https://www.westminstermint.com/

APPENDIX D

Crypto-Currencies

TrueNotes like Bit-Coin, Light-Coin and multiple other internet crypto-currencies can be purchased anonymously and saved or used online by trading with others or used to purchase goods and services provided by other holders of TrueNotes or businesses that accept them. TrueNotes however, are unique among them all.

Most crypto-currencies are very similar to real world currencies in that they are basically "Fiat Money" Systems where the currency is being used as a Medium of Exchange. What these currencies have in common is that they have no intrinsic value of their own. In and of themselves they are basically worthless. Their only value lay in the fact that others accept them. In other words it's a matter of faith that since accepted today hopefully tomorrow.

For Government Currencies their acceptance is a matter of decree by the Government making them legal tender and offering little other choice. Since some Medium of Exchange is necessary for commerce to occur, when government restricts the option to their currency reluctant or not people use it to conduct business with each other. For internet crypto-currencies it is the convenience of online trade along with certain attributes of decentralization, anonymity, popularity and investment possibility if not gambling itself.

With government currencies risks to the holders of such currency comes in the form of lost value through inflation, the over-printing of the currency, or in deflation the under printing of the currency. One hurts the value of your Money the other the value of your goods and labor. This constant manipulation steals from the People and lines the pockets of Politicians and Money Men.

Crypto-Currencies have become popular especially those that are decentralized, preventing such supply manipulation. The attribute of the holder being anonymous is also a big draw. Both these attributes are certainly frowned upon by governments and their tax authorities. This is leading to regulation and control by many states at the point in the system where these crypto-currencies seek exchange back into government currencies. At these points the stripping away of anonymity and review of tax implications occur.

This being the case these attributes are only advantages for holders of crypto-currencies willing to remain in and confine their transactions to the particular crypto-currencies selected. As such controls tighten the willingness to remain totally vested in a particular crypto-currency will depend greatly on its popularity, security and its various places of acceptance. This will tend to a consolidation of only the best and most popular leaving big losses for those holders last to abandon the less popular crypto-currencies.

Today's popular crypto-currencies seek subscribers by totting the fact that by setting strict limits on coin creation formulas, from yearly to lifetime maximums, that they remove the drawback of supply manipulation inherent with government currencies. But do they?

There is little question that their intent is more noble than that of Central Bankers and their Currencies. The problem lies in the arbitrary choice of the ultimate quantities of each coin and rate at which it is introduced. For a better and more complete understanding about Money especially "Fiat Money" and the schemes and problems caused by manipulation of its Supply you should read "What About Money" by Scott Dion. For now the abridged version is that the Supply of the Medium of Exchange if excessive leads to devaluation of the currency which means people require more of it if they are going to accept it at all, which means rising prices for goods and services. If on the other hand the Supply of it is lacking the scarceness of it will cause it to become more valuable meaning prices of goods and labor will go down to compete for it.

The above reactions to over or under supply of the Medium of Exchange (Money) are typical when it comes to government currencies because typically there is little choice with regard to having to use it one way or the other due to government decree. However, with internet crypto-currencies consumers have choices.

They can forgo participation altogether or move to one of many alternatives available to them. Although popularity may carry the day for a period of time neither the devaluing of the coin nor the devaluing of goods and labor will be tolerated by the majority for very long.

A popular crypto-currency whose value is rising will certainly attract speculators hoping to get in on the gains and will certainly hold those who get in early from leaving for similar reasons but will eventually discourage new-comers; believing it is too expensive and that they have missed the boat already. Additionally this leads to stagnant commerce since few want to part with what may become more valuable. This makes the coin more desirable than the goods it can buy. This may be a good attribute for an investment but is lousy as a Medium of Exchange (Money).

For one, few want to part with it and two those merchants selling goods get tired of getting less and less of it for what they are selling. This will eventuality lead to a different Medium of Exchange becoming used for commerce and an eventual collapse of the so-called crypto-currency that has been serving as more of an investment than an alternative currency.

The rise in value above occurred due to the under-supply of the particular crypto-currency this occurs when Demand for it is greater than its availability. Over-supply occurs when you have more coins or crypto-currency than people are currently demanding. In a government currency this is the reason for inflation. Since there is so much of it the cost of it is low sometimes pennies. Prices of goods measured by it are high because the merchant requires so much more of it before he is willing to part with the goods being sold.

In crypto-currency the cheaper price per coin may attract some speculators hoping they are getting in on the ground floor of the next great investment. It may also attract some not willing to pay the high prices of the more popular coin that they may think they missed the boat on. But so long as over-supply persists no matter how hopeful the investor its value will not rise significantly. Consequently merchants will maintain very high prices for their goods compared to it, if they will accept it at all.

As explained above over or under supply of a crypto-currency or coin has nothing to do with the number of them in existence, either currently or ultimately. It has to do with Supply of them in relationship to the Demand for them at any given time. As demonstrated neither an over-supply or an under-supply is a good thing for a Medium of Exchange (Money). Governments and Central Bankers get away with such circumstances due to the lack of alternatives their citizens have.

As an internet commodity the crypto-currencies are essentially just another product or good being sold to the consumer. A good totted as an alternative Medium of Exchange (Money). For the most part they are not even a real good, just like paper currency they are virtually worthless, without the faith and acceptance of others, they have no intrinsic value of their own.

Essentially crypto-currencies have been around for a few centuries now, they just called them something different. What is that? Stock in a Corporation. That's right I could open a Corporation today called Crypto Coin, Inc. and issue a million shares of stock and attempt to sell each share for one dollar. If the shares started selling like candy I could limit sales to one share per week and watch people bid up the Price to crazy amounts. If no one was interested at a dollar a share I would drop the Price to fifty cents or even lower if necessary. Purchasers would be free to sell them, hold them or trade them with each other or turn them in at an exchange for their current value. This happens everyday at the New York Stock Exchange and many others around the world.

So what's the difference? Only a couple of things. Today to do this with stock requires following Security Exchange Commission laws and selling stock to consumers in this fashion today is against the law. But go on the internet call your company a crypto-currency and nick name your stock some type of coin and "wallah" no current regulations to follow! Is it any different than buying Apple, Microsoft or IBM stocks and then going around using their value to buy or trade things? Well yes it is different, these stocks actually have a value in possible dividends as well as a divisional share in the Companies Asset Value where crypto-coins have no value above the current faith of others, placed in them.

Now that you are armed with a more complete picture of the things that should be considered in your decision to select a Medium of Exchange to use as a Money alternative it should becoming clearer that a proper Medium of Exchange should not be over-supplied nor under-supplied. Ideally it should equal Demand which the book "What About Money" will fully demonstrate. The result is steady value in the Medium of Exchange as well as the goods and labor being exchanged. Value is required to enter the system and anyone leaving the system removes their value when they exit. This makes for a self-governing Supply and Demand Ratio of the Medium of Exchange in the system. This causes everyone's interest to be protected.

The Medium that fits closest to the ideal Medium both for internet and real world use today hands down is TrueNotes. TrueNotes can be carried in your TrueNotes Wallet and used online to pay for the goods and services of other TrueNotes Wallet holders. TrueNotes have intrinsic value of their own unlike any other crypto-currency or coin, because they are backed by the deposits of real Gold, and Silver. These precious metals have intrinsic value and will never become worthless items. That means TrueNotes will never be worthless. Even if you were the last holder of them and everyone else jumped on the bandwagon of some new fad your TrueNotes will be redeemable (exchangeable) for the actual Gold, or Silver backing them.

That means online or off your TrueNotes will maintain value and be desired by someone no matter the changing fad or opinions of others. Anytime you want out of TrueNotes you can exchange them for the equivalent gold weight backing them. TrueNotes will never be the cause of Price inflation because there are never more in the system than are being Demanded. They will never cause Price deflation because they will not be under-supplied by declared time or quantity limits. This does not make them too easy to come by because the value of the intrinsically valued Gold or Silver backing them needs to be brought into the warehouse for them to be issued. Anytime someone leaves the system by taking their Gold or Silver the TrueNotes backed by those precious metals are retired (canceled). This means the proper ratio of Supply to Demand remains constant.

This means you can have all the convenience of any one of the many internet crypto-currencies or coins without their drawbacks and risks of loss. At the same time maintaining a Medium of Exchange also accepted anywhere in the world.

Aquaregics, LLC (Coupon for One 1 OZ Gold Bullion Coin)

Visit https://Aquaregics.com and receive an One Ounce Gold Bullion Coin for 1% below spot price with proof of purchase of "What About Money" by Scott Dion.
(Limit 1 Coin per purchase of "What About Money")

(https://whataboutmoney.org)

Coupon # 2022P0601

Made in the USA
Middletown, DE
12 June 2022

66890124R00119